RAW TALKS WITH WISDOM
MIKE PASCHALL

NOT YOUR GRANDMA'S DEVO

volume 4
OCTOBER, NOVEMBER, DECEMBER

RAW TALKS WITH WISDOM - *Not Your Grandma's Devo*
Volume 4 - *(October, November & December).*

Copyright © 2013, 2018 by Michael D. Paschall.

All rights reserved. No part of this book may be reproduced or stored in a retrieval system, or transmitted in any form or by any means—electronic, mechanical, photocopying, recording, or otherwise, without the written permission of owner.

FIRST EDITION

ISBN: 978-0-578-43991-4

Cover & Title Page: Jon C. Egan

EVERY TRIBE INTERNATIONAL
Colorado Springs, Colorado

www.everytribeinternational.org
mike@mikepaschall.com

CONTENTS

Preface   v

Dedication   ix

OCTOBER   1 - 50

NOBEMBER   53 - 103

DECEMBER   107 - 156

Endnotes   159

Resources & Other Helps   163

Acknowledgements   169

Author   173

PREFACE

HEY! Thank you so much for giving **RAW TALKS WITH WISDOM – *Not Your Grandma's Devo*** a whirl! It's an honor and a blessing to have you along for the ride. Before we get started, I thought it would be helpful to give you an idea of what this thing is all about.

FOUNDATIONS

Setting aside time every day for a devotional is probably one of the best disciplines I was ever encouraged to implement into my daily life. It has provided me countless connections with the Lord.

For the past 35 years, I have primarily read devotionals by two men, Dr. James Sidlow Baxter and Oswald Chambers. I was introduced to Dr. Baxter in 1978 by my first real spiritual mentor: Dr. H. D. McCarty. I heard Brother Sidlow speak on more than one occasion. He was already in his late '70s by the time I was introduced to his written work. I will always be thankful for **AWAKE MY HEART**. I learned so much from the meditations in that devotional.

Our friends, Earl and Barbara Patrick, gave me my first copy of **MY UTMOST FOR HIS HIGHEST** by Oswald Chambers when I was ordained in April 1986. I still use that same copy. I can't begin to describe the blessing that devotional has been to me. Chambers' revelations are amazing, especially considering he was only 43 years old when he died in 1917. His wife, Biddy, compiled transcripts and notes that eventually evolved into **UTMOST**, first published in 1927. I am forever in debt to them both for what was spoken, captured, and put into print for all of us to benefit.

MY DESIRE

My prayer is that the Lord will speak to you through **RAW TALKS WITH WISDOM – *Not Your Grandma's Devo*.** I have always gained wisdom and perspective by reading scripture and devotionals, but more important to me has been how the Holy Spirit tailors each lesson to fit my life. It doesn't really mean anything unless we can practically apply truth to the joys and tears of the now.

If all you come away with after working through these devotionals is more knowledge, then I'd have to really evaluate if it was all worth it. I would encourage you to take it to another level, beyond mere theology and theory, into the realms of practical reality--stuff you can wear, taste, and feel. I want you to know He gave you revelation!

MY VISION

It's simple. Do this devotional the way you would do any other devotional. But what I really want is for these daily lessons to stimulate journaling (which is the reason for the **"In the Pages"** questions at the end of each day). I would encourage you to make an appointment to meet with the Lord each day, and then stick with it. Daily appointments can become healthy habits in a relatively short period of time. Pick a time each day that "works" best for you, and make Him a priority!

I want the material to stick with you. I want you to chew on it throughout your day. I want you to discuss it over coffee with a friend or colleague. Stuff like that. My ultimate prayer is that ***RAW TALKS WITH WISDOM – Not Your Grandma's Devo*** adds value to your quiet times with the Lord!

Like I said, I want you to do this devotional the way you do devotionals. But here is the method I would use to tackle each day:

First, read the **entire chapter** of Proverbs for that day. If the day is June 11, then read all of Proverbs chapter 11.

Then read the focus verses that begin each devo.

Third, read the devotional itself.

Fourth, journal your responses to the **In The Pages** questions at the end, along with anything else you feel compelled to write about. Get yourself a good leather-bound journal! Your thoughts and prayers deserve a proper container.

Lastly, spend some time in prayer and meditation.

That is the vision.

I sincerely hope the Holy Spirit will speak to you through these devotionals and give you things to write about in your journal. I also hope these devotionals will get you in the habit of reading through all of Proverbs twelve times in one year. For as long as I have been soaking in Proverbs, I have found a surprise almost every time! A new perspective, a nugget of value, something I've never seen before. It has to be the Holy Spirit that does that, and so far, I love the process!

WHY *RAW TALKS WITH WISDOM* – *Not Your Grandma's Devo*?

It dawned on me one day that our relationships with the Lord should always be raw. I was stuck in the rut of religious activity for far too long! What I have with Him now feels very real, relaxed, and extremely relevant.

I live and work in a culture that is filled with young and old ideas. I have definitely mellowed over the years and learned how to slow down. I think this season is teaching me to be more focused on the stuff that actually counts. To say it, whatever "it" really is, without apology and with serious conviction.

I'm not a theologian. I know that. So there is no use in my trying to be one. I'm a weird mixture of stuff with a rich experience of failure and profound grace. ***RAW TALKS WITH WISDOM – Not Your Grandma's Devo*** is a title that feels like me. It gives me permission to be myself and say things like I really do.

I know the angels won't sing along to every single one of these devotionals for you. But maybe, just maybe, some of it will help someone, somewhere, turn and embrace the **RAW** truth of God's wisdom.

Michael D. Paschall
2013

For those who follow.

Leopard Poop

October 1
Proverbs 1

"The fear of the Lord is the beginning of knowledge: But fools despise wisdom and instruction." Proverbs 1:7, KJV

If there's one verse in Proverbs most of us can quote, it's this one. I would say this is a good one to memorize, because it sets the tone for the rest of the book.

The *"beginning,"* or the **rê'shîyth** (pronounced *ray-sheeth'*) meaning, *"the first in place, time, order and rank of wisdom and knowledge,"* is that we: *"fear the lord"*.

There are three different kinds of fear: **dread and terror** (Jonah 1:10), **to stand in awe** (1 Kings 3:38), and **reverence and respect** (Leviticus 19:3). God's heart would appeal to the polar opposite of dread and terror.

We should be motivated by our love and passion to please the Lord because we revere and respect Him. To live with this belief that God is just waiting around for us to mess up so he can invoke His death sentence is to miss the heart of God. Unfortunately, too many people live with this misguided and unhealthy fear.

God is love. Could we at least try to remember that?

Today's proverb also says that fools do not heed any of those concerns: *"but fools despise wisdom."* What does that mean?

The Hebrew verb **bûwz** (pronounced *booz*) means *"to disrespect, to have contempt, to disregard and treat as worthless."* Some commentators point out that the deeper issue is inside of the fool. There would be a glimmer of hope for the fool if his attitude was impermanent, something that could be corrected with discipline. But Proverbs says that discipline is wasted on the fool who won't listen.

The fool is a fool through and through, because he or she has no consideration or desire for doing what is pleasing to anyone else, including the Lord! For the fool, **pleasing self** is the preeminent response to everything.

Therefore, you can expect the fool to act a certain way, because his history, his present, and his future actions will be aligned with the disrespect that is in his heart. The prophet Jeremiah said,

"Can the Ethiopian change his skin or the leopard his spots? Then you also can do good who are accustomed to doing evil" (Jeremiah 13:23, NASB).

You can paint over a leopard's spots, but it's still a leopard. His leopard nature will still rule his ways. It's the same with the fool; he'll always leave a trail of leopard poop.

I'll let you draw some of your own conclusions here, but take a few moments to read about a young man's disrespect and total ignorance in a single moment that changed his life (Genesis 25:19-34).

How quickly and easily did Esau hand over one of the most precious things he had going for him?

"Thus Esau despised his birthright." (Genesis 25:34, NASB)

Wisdom is calling us to another dimension of living. It is a charge to set aside the ridiculous possibilities of trashing our inheritances, a mandate to live and do for the righteous causes of the Kingdom. We have to make a decision.

In The Pages

What do you believe it really means to *"fear the Lord"*? Read Romans 1:28 and 2 John 1:7, and write your own commentary.

Lambanō

October 2
Proverbs 2

"My son, if you receive my words, and treasure my commands within you..." Proverbs 2:1, NKJV

There are few words more meaningful than these: *"receive"* and *"treasure"*.

The Hebrew word for *"receive"* is **lâqach** (pronounced *law-kakh'*), and it means, *"to take."* Its implications are as wide as you can imagine—*"accept, bring, buy, carry away, drawn, fetch, get, reserve, seize, etc."* This Hebrew word specifies not what you receive, but instead drips with personal aggression.

There is a very similar word, **leqach** (pronounced *leh'-kakh*), reserved more for intellectual grasping of a doctrine or teaching. My point in mentioning this is that the wider use of **lâqach** allows for us to *receive* much, as we would any tangible object. We possess it, we own it, we have command over it and knowledge of its value, and we have the power to use the object as we see fit, allowing it to benefit others and ourselves.

The Hebrew word for *"treasure"* is **tsâphan** (pronounced *tsaw-fan'*) from the root meaning, *"to hide by covering over"*; the implication is *"to hoard or reserve; protect, to keep in a secret place."* It's this magnificent idea that we *treasure*, or put in a safe place, something of great value until a later time. Much like a trust fund, a savings account, or even a stockpile of canned goods in the basement, we access our treasure as needs (both expected and unexpected) arise.

Most spiritual discipline is validated by these same fiscal concepts.

You do today in preparation for tomorrow.

Its not all harvest and feasting year-round. Winter eventually comes, and it usually arrives before we are totally prepared. Make hay while you can make hay! You're going to need it!

Receive and treasure wisdom!

I can't think of the word *"receive"* without looking back on some of the instruction of Jesus. Jesus frequently used the word **lambanō** (pronounced *lam-ban'-o*), which means, *"to get a hold of or seize"* (Matthew 19:29; Mark 12:38-40; Luke 7:22; John 14:3).

One of the most significant uses came after the whole open-tomb phenomenon. The disciples were freaking out! Was it all just a sham? Is this how it was supposed to all go down?

Morale was completely obliterated! Then, suddenly, He appears in their midst, *"Peace be with you,"* as He shows them the scars. Then our Savior says again, *"Peace be with you; as the Father has sent Me, I also send you.' And when He had said this, He breathed on them and said to them, '****Receive*** *the Holy Spirit'"* (John 20:21-22, NASB).

Some scholars say these guys were already converted believers (John 15:3). This particular *"receiving"* was for anointing and power to go do the work of the Kingdom. I submit to you that they did indeed *receive* the presence, the person, and the unlimited power of the Holy Spirit!

The *effectiveness* of their going out was dependent upon the *extensiveness* of their *"receiving"*. It's still the same today for us!

In The Pages

Take some time to thank God for what you have received from Him! What is the last thing He downloaded to you? How has it affected your life?

Health and Wealth

October 3
Proverbs 3

"Don't assume that you know it all. Run to God! Run from evil! Your body will glow with health, your very bones will vibrate with life! Honor God with everything you own; give him the first and the best. Your barns will burst, your wine vats will brim over." Proverbs 3:7-10, MSG

Usually when we hear the words "**health and wealth**" in regards to the spiritual, we tend to roll our eyes. There isn't a whole lot of tolerance for prosperity theology, unless you're into the whole prosperity movement and you've structured your life around that kind of teaching.

Maybe the whole televised version of this stuff is what turns people's stomach. You see these guys on television promising you all kinds of blessings if you just get out your checkbook.

Despite how some people have perverted it, scripture is full of all kinds of promises for our good health and provision!

Truth is truth, even when people use that truth for less than admirable purposes. We need to approach it with an open mind. Not everyone who preaches "health and wealth" is going to use your money to make a payment on their private jet. Don't judge the entire lot based on the eschewed few.

To *"honor God with everything you own"* is not the same thing as throwing your money at God, trying to cut a deal for a new Lexus. There is no "bargaining" with God.

I assure you, He doesn't need your money. Martin Luther lost his mind over this stuff. We don't make business transactions with the Lord. Want to know why Jesus flipped over the moneychanger's tables? It was a strong message:

No more buying and selling of God!

Honor requires a right heart. He knows the difference, remember? He is not moved by our outward responses. He is all about what is happening under the hood... inside our heart.

What if that's true? What if *"honor God with everything you own"* is directly tied to *"your body will glow with health, your very bones will vibrate with life,"* like the scripture says?

I truly believe spiritual health and natural health are related (Proverbs 3:8; 12:4; 14:30; 15:30; 16:24; 17:22). People who are spiritually happy are usually naturally happy.

Spiritual lovers tend to make easy transitions to loving mankind. The people who honor God, and love their brothers and sisters on this planet, are usually people of impeccable character and vigor. They *glow* everywhere they go, because they are full of life!

Today's text is not a promise that Camelot awaits our every decision and life encounter. It's just a reminder that serving and honoring God with our time, our energy, our gifts, our money, our families, and ultimately everything we have, generates a current that affects our natural and spiritual good. It's not just another formula to get what we want.

Besides, do we really want everything that we think we want?

In The Pages

Have you ever tried to cut a deal with God? What did you offer? What was it you wanted? How did it turn out for you? Are you convinced of God's response?

Right Paths

October 4
Proverbs 4

"I have taught you in the way of wisdom; I have led you in right paths. When you walk, your steps will not be hindered, and when you run, you will not stumble." Proverbs 4:11-12, NKJV

This feels like something a dad would say to his 20-year-old son (or daughter). There is no elementary instruction here. This is definitely not child's play.

It all seems to flow more out of prophetic encouragement. This whole ideal of walking securely and then progressing into an unimpeded run is an idiom called "anabasis." The increase of progress and speed actually strengthens the subject to the point of being almost invincible.

It would have to make your heart skip a beat to hear your dad invoke such spiritual authority and prophetic unction over your life!

Some of us are still trying to figure out how to get our father's applause and notice. A father's blessing is a powerfully spiritual dynamic for every one of us! People who never got that blessing usually struggle with identity and self-confidence.

Or we drive ourselves, trying to earn applause from anyone and everyone we can. But nothing parallels the blessing and confirmation we get from our fathers! Even Father God made sure we all heard Him bless His Son at Jesus' baptism (Matthew 3:17). It's a spiritual dynamic that's probably much more important than we ever realize.

So what is Solomon really saying here? I mean, it sounds good and all, but is there any truth to what he is saying to his son?

The *"way of wisdom"* is an invite from the Lord to walk (our hand in His hand) through life with us. David said,

"Yes, because God's your refuge, the High God your very own home, evil can't get close to you, harm can't get through the door. He ordered his angels to guard you wherever you go. If you stumble, they'll catch you; their job is to keep you from falling. You'll walk unharmed among lions and snakes, and kick young lions and serpents from the path" (Psalms 91:9-13, MSG).

I once heard a renowned prophet mention that we have 250,000 angels at our disposal[1]. They're all waiting around for us to give them something to do! I'm not sure where the old seer got that number, but if he is anywhere in the ballpark, that is quite a bit of help!

Solomon and David remind us that God isn't squeamish about getting involved in our lives. In fact, He is willing and able to fully engage in our affairs, desires, and passions for living. He'll also check in when we are hurting, sick, lonely, and fearful! Not that He fixes everything, but He'll be there with us.

Before He ascended, Jesus said to His disciples, *"These things I have spoken to you, so that in Me you may have peace. In the world you have tribulation, but take courage; I have overcome the world"* (John 16:33, NASB).

We can take comfort with this because it's those who understand our battles, and have also won their own wars, who bring the most sound help and advice when we are in the thick of it! HE has overcome, and HE wants the same for us!

In The Pages

When is the last time you genuinely felt that God had intervened and helped you out of a tight jam? How much thanks did you offer Him? What is your take on Romans 8:31?

Milk and Honey

October 5
Proverbs 5

"For the lips of the adulterous woman drip honey, and her seductive words are smoother than olive oil, but in the end she is bitter as wormwood, sharp as a two-edged sword. Her feet go down to death; her steps lead straight to the grave." Proverbs 5:3-5, NET

"Your lips, my bride, drip honey; honey and milk are under your tongue, and the fragrance of your garments is like the fragrance of Lebanon." Song of Solomon 4:11, NASB

The longer I hang out in Proverbs, the more grateful I am for the divine and sacred institution of marriage.

God really knew what He was doing when he hardwired us!

Really, it is beyond words trying to understand, let alone explain, all of the mystical, spiritual, emotional, and sexual goodness that comes from the union between a man and a woman. After 35 plus years of marriage, I couldn't agree more with Solomon's Song!

The romance and seduction that take place within the margins of marital covenant are truly the stuff of *milk and honey*! When it's right, oh how the angels sing, dear brothers and sisters! Or, you can choose to color outside the lines of His caring boundaries and find out for yourself what today's proverb is all about.

She (the spirit of adultery) romances and seduces, but the end result is NOT *milk* and *honey*. Time spent with an *adulterous* man or woman leads to less that favorable results.

The word for *"wormwood"* is **laʻănâh** (pronounced *lah-an-aw'*), also known as *"hemlock."* According to Strong's Concordance, it is *"a kind of curse, poison, gall, or bitterness."* The hemlock plant is a weed found in the Middle East that has a sickly sweet aroma, but to ingest it is poison to us.

Another telling image of the adulterer is that of the *"two-edged sword."* Whichever way the sword moves, it cuts and slices deeply and efficiently. It's the kind of sharpness that can divide between bone and marrow. That sort of sharpness can do quite a bit of damage with very little effort.

I guess one could dissect this passage all day long, but let's just say what is real here:

Outside of the covenant of marriage, fooling around with an adulterer provokes an invitation to death and misery, not life.

"Her [or his] *feet go down to death; her steps lead straight to the grave"* (Proverbs 5:5, NET).

Where is life in this? Where? There is no *milk* and *honey*! There is no joy in this! This is nothing but a frolic with witchcraft!

Lovers, stay in love with your mate! Taste and enjoy the *milk* and *honey* that God has given you!

In The Pages

Couples, when is the last time you made a big deal out of a date night? Even if you have small children, you must date! You must get away (without the kids)! Be creative and find ways to sow into your marital intimacy! Work it out! Make it happen! Look at your calendar and plan a focused weekend for you and your lover!

Real Sex Ed

October 6
Proverbs 6

"My son, observe the commandment of your father and do not forsake the teaching of your mother; bind them continually on your heart; tie them around your neck. When you walk about, they will guide you; when you sleep, they will watch over you; and when you awake, they will talk to you." Proverbs 6:20-22, NASB

Where I come from, "tying one on," means something totally different from what Solomon is talking about here. The words *"bind"* and *"tie"* send a strong message. It was the Jewish attempt to literally fulfill part of the law.

It was very common to see serious religious men walking around with all kinds of religious paraphernalia tied to their person. We'll come back to this later.

If you wanted to make a case for sex education in the home, this would be a good place to start. Today's focus verses are the start of a 15-verse caution on sexual mismanagement of body and soul.

While the counsel is wise, I get a sense most Christian parents get a little squeamish talking about this kind of stuff with our adolescents and pubescent juveniles. Even if you think your teen is already active, you still have to talk to them!

There has to be real dialogue between parents and children.

We need to start talking about real stuff with them. Believe me, our kids are hearing "the basics" earlier than anyone would expect. Handing your son a condom and a pat on the back and telling him to be careful is like throwing a novice driver into rush-hour traffic!

A kid needs to hear words like *"honor"* and *"inheritance."*

Parents, isn't that what we're supposed to do? Teaching them the physiological stuff while ignoring the emotional and spiritual dynamics of sexuality is asking for trouble. There is more to sexuality than plumbing. We have to do better!

The salutation *"my son"* is marinated in love. Dad isn't being a control freak. He loves his kids, and he doesn't want to see them involved in regrettable situations that landmine safe paths.

He is willing to talk candidly. So is mom. The son or daughter is asked to "*bind them* [these teachings] *continually on your heart.*"

The word for *"bind"* is **qâshar** (pronounced *kaw-shar´*) meaning, *"to gird or knit together in love."* It conveys covenantal and mystical unification in the heart. Then he says, *"tie them around your neck,"* as you would a medallion or amulet. Visualize a rope or metal chain with an ornament hanging loosely near the heart. It's great imagery!

It is a wise parent who invests deeply in his child's welfare. He's not afraid of the big stuff. Love is the driving force, and he risks temporary discomfort for long-term dividends.

Read the rest of the chapter. You'll see the man is trying to keep his son or daughter out of reckless pain and heartache. We should all love that much!

In The Pages

You know your own story better than anyone. How prepared were you to face your own sexuality? If applicable, how are you preparing yourself to talk to your own kids? What values do you want them to know? Why?

Fatal Attractions

October 7
Proverbs 7

Soon she has him eating out of her hand, bewitched by her honeyed speech. Before you know it, he's trotting behind her, like a calf led to the butcher shop, like a stag lured into ambush and then shot with an arrow, like a bird flying into a net not knowing that its flying life is over." Proverbs 7:21-23, MSG

It might be a gift, I'm not really sure, but early on in my pursuit of God, I found that when I read scripture, I was able to move emotionally into the scene. I can hear and see all kinds of things along with the imagery laid out by the text.

I guess you can call it imagination or whatever you want, but it happens quite a bit when I'm studying. It helps me to "get inside" what's just under the surface... behind the curtain. Today's text is one of those scenes. I feel a dad's weighty concern for his kid's welfare.

Here we have the man who prayed for wisdom from God. As he has grown into knowledge and accumulated wealth, he now finds himself focused on "paying it forward" to the next generation.

King Solomon lays out three disturbing images: *"Calf led to the butcher shop,"* *"stag... shot with the arrow,"* and *"the (free) bird flying into a net."* He is alluding to the potential hazards of illicit sexual liaisons in all three.

The NASB uses the word *"suddenly"* in verse 22. Whatever bait was used to lure in its victim... it worked. Something sweet for the calf, corn for the deer, and fresh worm for the bird—the end result is fatal. They took the bait and fell prey to the captivity awaiting them.

All of these things were kid games. Just typical ways of passing time, having fun—just doing the things kids do. Solomon is showing us how easily it all goes down. See the bait, smell the bait, touch the bait...suddenly you're trapped. It's the bitter reality of just how fast things that seem harmless can turn ugly!

I think of that 1980's movie *Fatal Attraction* with Michael Douglas and Glenn Close. What an appropriate title! Other than having to see some really bad '80s hairstyles, it was worth the view.

A happily married man with a great job and a great family considers an "innocent" sexual affair with another woman. It begins like most "innocent" affairs do, but then it turned into a horrific nightmare for his entire family!

I don't think we should chalk this thing up to Hollywood. It's a prophetic statement about what happens when we linger around the bait too long. There is death inside of that *"suddenly!"*

Like a trapped bird, the freedom is gone. Like a harnessed calf, the butcher's knife awaits. Like the unsuspecting trophy deer, the noose traps and holds it until the archer can move close enough to deal the deadly blow through its viscera of life.

In The Pages

How do you feel emotionally when you read all of this? What warnings sound in your head and heart? Do you think Solomon was just being dramatic? What do you think were his real desires in this passage?

Turds in the Punchbowl

October 8
Proverbs 8

"The fear of the Lord is to hate evil; pride and arrogance and the evil way and the perverse mouth I hate." Proverbs 8:13, NKJV

What does it really mean to *"fear the Lord?"* We know the fear of the Lord is the beginning of knowledge (Proverbs 1:7). In fact, it's the beginning of wisdom.

Today's proverb shows us some other characteristics that manifest when we *fear the Lord.* Now, it's usually bad form for us Christians to be hatin' on anything. It gets in the way of our religious facades. It's out of place... like floaties in the punch.

Still, most of us are usually in disagreement with evil—crooked, perverse, twisted destruction that negates all trust and releases "bad seed" into the spirit realm. Even those who are not living in a "spirit savvy" environment get this.

Bad words, evil acts, rotten energy, all produce soiled fruit. *"The fear of the Lord"* should arouse **sânê'** (pronounced *saw-nay'*) in us. It's a much stronger word than *dislike*. In this context, *"hate"* is the internal aggression inside our heart that rejects any notion or activity of wickedness.

Church culture loves to define *"evil"* for us. We have to understand that *evil* goes much deeper than deviant behavior. What's the source of the behavior? What's causing this *evil* display? What's behind our crappy attitudes and nastiness?

Two words that pretty much negate most spiritual productivity in the world today are: *"pride"* and *"arrogance."* When these two things are involved, it destroys the Spirit of Christ in that particular environment. It absolutely absolves unity. It scatters faith. It replaces freedom with things like control and religion, releasing the spirit of Jezebel to do her destructive work.

*"For all that is in the world, the lust of the flesh and the lust of the eyes and the **boastful pride of life**, is not from the Father, **but is from the world**" (1 John 2:16, NASB).*

The biggest problem with pride is that we are usually the last one to see it in ourselves.

Trust me, everyone around you sees it, and if you're trying to promote the Kingdom while wearing the garments of *arrogant pride*, you have become the antithesis to your purpose. I speak from my own gruesome personal experience.

To Hezekiah's credit, he knew his God was different from the wooden/metal idols Sennacherib surrounded himself with. Hezekiah's God was alive and attentive to his heart and request for Israel. So he petitions God for favor against his foe. Isaiah brings the King a word. Again, we get to see what God sees and hear what He wants us to reject:

"'Because of your raging against Me, and because your **arrogance** *has come up to My ears, therefore I will put My hook in your nose, and My bridle in your lips, and I will turn you back by the way which you came"* (2 Kings 19:28, NASB).

God still has an opinion about *arrogant pride*. Agreed?

In The Pages

What are some characteristics of arrogant pride? What is the difference between pride and confidence? Is there such a thing as righteous pride? How thin is the line between the two? How would you know if you crossed that line?

Mess'n with "ME" Monsters

October 9
Proverbs 9

"If you reason with an arrogant cynic, you'll get slapped in the face; confront bad behavior and get a kick in the shins. So don't waste your time on a scoffer; all you'll get for your pains is abuse. But if you correct those who care about life, that's different—they'll love you for it!" Proverbs 9:7-8, MSG

I like movies that mess with me. Stephen Spielberg's *"Shindler's List"* is a perfect example. If you haven't seen it, it's definitely worth checking out, but please note that it's not for the faint of heart.

The setting is World War II, the Holocaust, when the German army sent millions of Polish-Jewish refugees to Auschwitz, a network of concentration and extermination camps. Spielberg, who is Jewish himself, did not spare us the gory details of what can only be described as a man-made hell.

Just know that to watch this film is to expose your heart and your spirit to something horrific. But the story is told wonderfully, and it will stretch your knowledge and open you emotionally to some of what these people went through.

In the movie, there is a scene where Oskar Schindler (a German businessman) is attempting to reason with Amon Göth (a Nazi officer) about the definition of power. Goth's character, played by Ralph Fiennes, had been senselessly exercising his military authority by randomly killing Jews for the smallest infractions, typically to send a message to others that he was a man to be feared and dreaded.

Schindler attempts to enlighten Goth in a private conversation that such brutality cannot really be defined as "power." He tells the heartless officer that real power manifests itself in the pardon and forgiveness of weakness. Shindler pressed that ultimate power has the ability to forgive error, thereby granting life, rather than taking it.

What Schindler says actually ends up changing the Nazi officer's behavior for a couple of days, though he ultimately succumbs to his own bestial instincts and resumes his savage killings with a greater fervor.

My point is that you can save yourself a lot of wasted time if you can determine whether or not the people you're talking to have an appreciation for what brings life. Try to discern what they value. Some people just have different value systems.

They don't care about anything out there that doesn't conform to their own ways and inclinations. The world is full of takers! Self-pleasing, me-focused living leaves little room for the voice of Wisdom.

What this proverb is saying is that we need to run some assessments, some "background checks," before we spill our pearls before ME-Monsters.

Cutting into another person's agenda, one that is not "others-focused," only means you will be the one demonized and berated with insults.

Living differently in their presence may have much more value and positive effect than trying to reason with the unreasonable. You can try, but take the proverbial baby steps.

Remember, they don't think they need your help or your wisdom. Cover this bad boy in some prayer before you jump in.

In The Pages

How patient are you? Before you swoop in to help or correct, do you put much thought in to your approach? Do you have to tell everything you know all at once, or are you able to parcel out bits of wisdom to see how it is received? How do you handle the hard cases?

Yackity Yack

October 10
Proverbs 10

"The wise of heart will receive commands, but a babbling fool will be ruined." Proverbs 10:8, NASB

"Therefore everyone who hears these words of Mine and acts on them, may be compared to a wise man who built his house on the rock. And the rain fell, and the floods came, and the winds blew and slammed against that house; and yet it did not fall, for it had been founded on the rock. Everyone who hears these words of Mine and does not act on them, will be like a foolish man who built his house on the sand. The rain fell, and the floods came, and the winds blew and slammed against that house; and it fell—and great was its fall." Matthew 7:24-27, NASB

"The wise of heart will receive commands, but a babbling fool will be ruined." Proverbs 10:8, NASB

"Therefore everyone who hears these words of Mine and acts on them, may be compared to a wise man who built his house on the rock. And the rain fell, and the floods came, and the winds blew and slammed against that house; and yet it did not fall, for it had been founded on the rock. Everyone who hears these words of Mine and does not act on them, will be like a foolish man who built his house on the sand. The rain fell, and the floods came, and the winds blew and slammed against that house; and it fell—and great was its fall." Matthew 7:24-27, NASB

Confession time. Today's proverb makes me reflect on my early years in ministry. I shudder to think what all those people I pastored must have thought of my shallow talk, religion, and narrow points of view. I didn't have enough life experience to be leading much of anything, especially mature spiritual people.

Some of the advice I gave was just that of a *"babbling fool."* Don't get me wrong; I had passion, which is probably why so much grace was extended to me. It sounds goofy, but I never planned to preach and teach in the first place. That was never a part of my plan.

I just wanted to work with youth, build Sunday school programs for teens, and be a good Baptist guy. God had other plans on all counts.

Looking back, I wish I had just kept my mouth shut more often. I wish I had listened more. Really listened. I'm pretty sure not much in this old world has changed because of my goofy babblings! It took me too long to figure out that *love* is the utmost form of communication. I have some regrets about all of that.

Solomon reminds us that Wisdom would have us in a posture of *receiving* instruction much more than a posture of broadcasting our ideas.

We're not great in living out this concept.

It is ok to give away what we have. But our help needs to come from a deeper place, a restful place—an experiential *knowing* place that God has breathed on.

In today's Matthew passage, Jesus tells us how important it is to have knowledge based on *hearing*. This is what gives us the kind of experience that makes it worth another person's time to hear what we have to say.

Spiritual theory is easily *thrown down*. The witness of your experience is what gives your words an anchor.

In The Pages

Ever been in a situation where you knew it was better to hush than to weigh in? How does it feel when you realize you talk too much? Do you like it when someone tells you how you feel?

Gazillionaire Plight

October 11
Proverbs 11

"Riches do not profit in the day of wrath, but righteousness delivers from death." Proverbs 11:4, NKJV

"A thick bankroll is no help when life falls apart, but a principled life can stand up to the worst." Proverbs 11:4, MSG

"Near is the great day of the Lord, near and coming very quickly; listen, the day of the Lord! In it the warrior cries out bitterly. A day of wrath is that day, a day of trouble and distress, a day of destruction and desolation, a day of darkness and gloom, a day of clouds and thick darkness, a day of trumpet and battle cry against the fortified cities and the high corner towers. I will bring distress on men so that they will walk like the blind, because they have sinned against the Lord; and their blood will be poured out like dust and their flesh like dung. Neither their silver nor their gold will be able to deliver them on the day of the Lord's wrath; and all the earth will be devoured in the fire of His jealousy, for He will make a complete end, indeed a terrifying one, of all the inhabitants of the earth." Zephaniah 1:14-18, NASB

No, I'm not trying to scare you awake today. I'm adding color to the word *"wrath."*

The Hebrew language has many different words for *"wrath."* The word used in both of today's focus verses is ʿ**ebrâh** (pronounced *eb-raw'*) meaning, *"outburst of passion, anger or rage."*

This is the stuff that fed The Great Awakening, and motivated sermons like *"Sinners in the Hands of an Angry God,"* by Jonathan Edwards. It was a sure-fire way to scare the hell out of you and get you to sign on the dotted line for righteous living. There were no margins. You were either "all in," or you were toast. Sadly, it was quite effective.

Historically, Zephaniah's prophecy bore fruit almost 25 years later, when Israel was basically enslaved by Babylonia, which involved King Nebuchadnezzar deporting almost 10,000 Jews. The numbers are staggering, but not nearly as sickening as the modern Holocaust.

Whether you give God credit or blame doesn't matter. My point is that our stuff can't save us. The word for *"riches"* means *"enough substance."*

Please hear me, this isn't a rebuke against having money and provision. I'm not singling out the wealthy or making any kind of statement against them. In America, you can be on welfare and still have more money than two-thirds of the world's population! By that standard, we are all frikk'n gazillionaires.

And we need to remember, it takes money to do ministry at home and abroad. There are no pots of gold under the rainbow. We need provision to make stuff happen in the Kingdom!

I think Peterson caught the real heart of today's Proverb. When *"life falls apart,"* we need more than money. Money doesn't buy courage or honor. Cash doesn't equate to peace. Strong portfolios can't guarantee righteousness and leverage in eternal currency.

Money is a tool, that's all. It is not our source.

In The Pages

Most really successful and wealthy individuals have been bankrupt at one time or another. What does that tell you about the stability of money? Please read Ecclesiastes 6:1-2 and Jeremiah 9:23-24. Take a moment and journal your thoughts.

Swords

October 12
Proverbs 12

"There is one who speaks rashly like the thrusts of a sword, but the tongue of the wise brings healing." Proverbs 12:18, NASB

My soul is among lions; I lie among the sons of men who are set on fire, whose teeth are spears and arrows, and their tongue a sharp sword. Be exalted, O God, above the heavens; let Your glory be above all the earth." Psalms 57:4-5, NASB

We've all done it, right? Acted out in those moments of frustration and anger where we've not only wounded others, but also inevitably damaged our own reputation?

The word for *"rashly"* is **bâṭâh** (pronounced *baw-taw'*), from the root word, *"babble."* Only in this case, it's the kind of *"babbling"* that's associated with anger, which has us speaking unadvisedly. It's reckless and thoughtless.

"The tongue also is a fire, a world of evil among the parts of the body. It corrupts the whole person, sets the whole course of his life on fire, and is itself set on fire by hell" (James 3:6, NIV).

Pastor James knew a thing or two. The man was responsible for the 1st church in Jerusalem. He understood the cost of living with the sheep in tight quarters and pasturing them, despite outside pressure.

He probably did more than his fair share of damage control within his community. I also find it interesting that the ancient Jews referred to the edge of a sword as the *"mouth."* Oh yeah, it can be very sharp!

"With the tongue we praise our Lord and Father, and with it we curse men, who have been made in God's likeness. Out of the same mouth come praise and cursing. My brothers, this should not be. Can both fresh water and salt water flow from the same spring? My brothers, can a fig tree bear olives, or a grapevine bear figs? Neither can a salt spring produce fresh water" (James 3:9-12, NASB).

What a mysteriously magnificent paradox! We can use the same instrument for completely opposite spectrums with equal ease and aptitude. What shall we choose?

Lady Wisdom appeals to our logic and passion:

"Choose words that project life and healing!"

I'm reminded of a night in Toronto (1997) when I was prophesied over by a big man I only knew as Jim. I have often been called out in corporate settings for "a word," but this was different. This time, I stood silently and waited to be approached by whoever dared.

Here he came with a head of moppy red hair, full of grace and sweet rest. I knew his words were opening me up, and I chose to allow the healing to happen. But his words didn't just open me up; they also cut me, broke me, and healed me... all at once. It was a significant moment I'll never forget.

There are times for swords. But it's time we gave some thought to the power of our words. Our hearts govern our tongues. Our focus should be on what brings more healing.

In The Pages

What part of today's teaching spoke to your spirit? Have you experienced the effects of rash words? What about healing words?

Hope Deferred = Sick Heart

October 13
Proverbs 13

"Hope deferred makes the heart sick, but when the desire comes, it is a tree of life." Proverbs 13:12, NKJV

Today I was thinking about how whatever mood I'm in affects these writings. I'm in one of those moods today where I want to sit down with young married men everywhere, grab a beer, light a cigar, and have a nice, long discussion about this verse.

My heart definitely gravitates towards sons, but I do not have natural sons. God blessed me with two natural daughters, and they have taught me a lot about myself.

I wasn't very good at fathering them early on, but they were patient and gracious with all of my blundering efforts. As they grew up, I grew up. They are what prepared me for leadership.

They taught me: without love... it's all pointless!

Our daughters (natural and spiritual) set standards and motivate us men to grow up into the full stature of manhood: warriors, princes, lovers of honor and selfless sacrifice. I have no problem whatsoever in seating one of the daughters (natural and spiritual) at the table with such fine company.

I recognize that the only reason I have spiritual sons is because they have made a choice to come under my headship and counsel. I have to admit, having sons who share in my passions and salute my life is quite the reward for the many years I have dedicated to ministry. They honor me much more than I probably deserve, and I take very seriously their desire for a place in my heart.

It really is a wonderful dynamic! Sons and daughters are truly a gift from the Lord! The fact that they want to be in my life makes my world a great place to live in!

Now, back to the beer, the cigar, and the discussion.

Too many young women are waiting for the men they've said "yes" to, to become the men they thought they said "yes" to.

Immature men make promises they can't keep, or that they have no intention of honoring. They live for the moment, regardless of what it costs them later.

"Hope deferred makes the heart sick."

Every woman has hope that her guy will be different from the rest. She has a fierce longing to feel protected and secure. She craves internal strength, mutual respect, and unconditional love.

A woman who does not respect her man is a *"heart sick"* woman! As I've already said, too many of God's daughters are waiting for the little boys inside of their men to diminish and for the real men to emerge.

The word *"deferred"* is **mâshak** (pronounced *maw-shak'*). Our vernacular would best describe it as *"the person who is dragging their feet, shuffling along, and basically wasting time."*

Any spiritually mature man would love to have the opportunity to tell this guy that it's time to grow up and put away the toys of self-centered pleasure. Stop dragging the baggage from your past into the opportunities of the present.

Sir, she is waiting on you.

In The Pages

Richard Rohr says, *"In order for a man to be born, the boyhood and keeping all my options open, must die. The man must use his sword to kill the boy inside."*[2] Elaborate on what you think all that means. A properly initiated man gets this. How would you suggest we convey this to the next generation?

It should be obvious that these devos come from my own personal experiences and relationships. I do not mean to disrespect or minimize anyone who might not totally identify with the traditional marital roles that I've described here. That holds true for every lesson in this book! The overall message is that deferred maturity is a frustrating thing in any serious relationship. If we love... we must change. That's the bottom-line of what I'm saying here. —MDP 2018

Backsliders

October 14
Proverbs 14

"The backslider in heart will have his fill of his own ways, but a good man will be satisfied with his." Proverbs 14:14, NASB

"Do not be deceived, God is not mocked; for whatever a man sows, this he will also reap. For the one who sows to his own flesh will from the flesh reap corruption, but the one who sows to the Spirit will from the Spirit reap eternal life. Let us not lose heart in doing good, for in due time we will reap if we do not grow weary." Galatians 6:7-9, NASB

It's a word I haven't really used in over twenty years:

BACKSLIDER.

It's what caught my eye today.

Honestly, I feel more condemnation when I hear this word than caution, only because I know how I've used this word in the past. It was a control word. Out of my own religious desire to see people act right or do what I wanted them to do, I would just play the "backslider" card and people started shaping up.

It was a quick way to profile the people who wouldn't conform to church rules, doctrine, or agenda. Who the heck wants to be labeled a backslider? Fortunately for us, Wisdom isn't coming from that same kind of nasty posture.

We are being reminded of the spiritual and natural laws of sowing and reaping. It's worth another look, even if you've labeled (or been labeled) that wicked backslider.

"Backslider" is **çûwg** (pronounced *soog*), and it means *"to flinch, to go back, to turn around; to actually use your progress to carve a way in the opposite direction."* It's a drifting from secure shores. Another example is when we use the good in our lives for harmful purposes. It may not be necessarily intentional, but it is a passionate influence nonetheless!

So here is where we get to it. If we choose to take that path of error, we are going to reap what we sow. *"The backslider in heart will have his fill..."* The NIV says he'll be *"fully repaid."* No matter how you translate it, you're going to get back what you've put out there. The same is true for the *"good man"*... a complete harvest from that which we sowed!

We see in the Book of Galatians a clear reminder of this. But context is everything!

Backtrack to the beginning of the Chapter 6. Paul is making a significant request to the church to not get caught up in judgment and profiling. The course they were to follow was the one Christ taught them all with His lifestyle.

Paul says it would be a detour for them (the Body) to declare themselves followers of Jesus, yet not offer love and support to brothers and sisters in Christ who have stumbled or fallen into bondage. To not love them rightly, to not risk restoration, to make pronouncements of soiled character producing stiff-armed tactics, makes *us* the *"backsliders"*, not the ones carrying shame for their past mistakes.

And when it comes to church leaders, it's harder to refrain from fronting out the distasteful methods that hold people in religious performance and bondage. We tire of bored preachers who cash it all in for cheap thrills, playing it safe, and cold soup.

Regardless, it's not right to point a finger! We all have to readjust in this area at whatever level we struggle. Why? Because reaping happens.

In The Pages

How do you feel about the backslider? Is it time you changed your mind? In what way? What is a better approach?

Straw Mats

October 15
Proverbs 15

"Fear-of-GOD is a school in skilled living—first you learn humility, then you experience glory." Proverbs 15:33, MSG

"The fear of the Lord is the instruction for wisdom, and before honor comes humility." Proverbs 15:33, NASB

Peter fit the mold for what you would expect from a typical pastor in Uganda.[3] Thin, soft-spoken, gentle, gracious, black as night, and very humble. That is, until you put a microphone in his hand and set him loose in front of a crowd!

He would then morph into this hyperactive, fire-breathing evangelist. The man would become electric, his energy pulsating through everyone within earshot.

Spending time with him meant visiting orphanages and schools he had started in the eastern part of the country. Hours of driving on rutted footpaths, which always led to some other thatch-roofed hut that was "church" to another 50 people. Peter was known everywhere!

This little man had a huge ministry that was both infectious and stealthy. People were buzzing around him constantly, taking orders and rushing around to help him accomplish his tasks. It was impressive, to say the least.

There is always a story behind a person.

Africa is a difficult place to evangelize. Where did this fire Peter breathed come from? I started asking questions.

"Oh Pastor Mike, God told me one day I would be responsible for many people. He said that I must first serve my pastor until he released me to my task. I slept for three years on a straw mat at the foot of his bed. I washed and ironed his clothes every day, I cooked his meals, and I carried his Bible everywhere he went. I was his shadow. I listened when he spoke, and I talked only when he asked me a question. I learned many valuable lessons by serving that man."

My head was reeling! He continued,

"Then, one day he came to me and said that God had told him it was time for me to go. He anointed me with oil, laid hands on me, and prayed a commission over my life. He said that I was now to serve the world the way I had served him. I have tried my best to do that ever since."

This is not the kind of humility we are accustomed to! Much of what we see in the western church flows more out of self-serving *entitlement* than real humility. Yet the very heart of *"honor"* is HUMILITY.

No one gets to skip that step.

That's what makes prideful displays of haughtiness among clergy and ministries so offensive. The Body also likes to think it honors its leaders, but there is a fine line between patronizing and honor. *"Humility"* is the difference.

If we could get this, it could possibly turn the way the world looks at the Church.

In The Pages

What does honor look like to you? How do you honor others? Have you ever experienced true humility in another person? What was its effect on you?

Hoary Glory

October 16
Proverbs 16

"The hoary head is a crown of glory, if it be found in the way of righteousness." Proverbs 16:31, KJV

Yeah, I went to Webster's on this one. I don't think I've ever used the word *"hoary"* before. I elected to use the King James Version, not because of this very cool word, but because this particular translation emanates an ideal the other translations do not. They're all close, but not the same.

The many years I've spent observing male spiritual growth have led me to the conclusion that a lot of the problems our young men have with the maturing process are due to the absence of a legitimate initiation rite. Self-initiation doesn't work. So when does a man start to become a man?

Women have an actual physiological change that happens to their bodies during adolescence, which is an obvious sign that they are transitioning from little girls to women. It's not that straightforward for men.

The whole benefit of an initiation process is to get an idea (upfront) on the inside of the initiate of where this thing is going, what is required, and what steps need to be taken to promote the overall objectives. This process is crucial to proper development in both men and women, and it helps us transfer fully to the next stage of growth.

It validates the "now" of the process, while continuing to point to the future as the ultimate goal. This is what today's text is talking about. It is a good thing when the *"hoary head,"* a mature man or woman, full of life experiences (both good and bad), commits to ways of righteousness that bring glory and honor to themselves, their families, and their God. Like I said earlier, I chose this translation because of the *"if"* in the text.

Hundreds of years ago, it was rare to see a really old person. Disease, lack of medical understanding, and harsher living conditions made it uncommon to live more than 60 years or so. So if you happened to meet someone past the ripe old age of 75, you had to assume he was doing something right and had God's hand directly on him.

Obviously, things have changed. Thanks to advancements in science and medicine, as a culture, we are getting older. Walk into any restaurant around 4 p.m. that has a senior discount. They'll be packed in there like sardines! My point? Just because it's more common to see people living longer these days, it does not guarantee *"glory"* or *"righteousness."*

The *"if"* in today's text is big.

A *"hoary head"* is someone who has learned valuable life lessons and who influences the kingdom by choosing to pass along these golden nuggets of truthful insight.

They realize their lives aren't about them. They're mature. They know life is hard and sometimes short. They choose to serve others anyway. They see the fence on the backside of their pasture.

They want to finish well before they enter into their reward! That is the proper translation: strength to wisdom, warrior to king, student to teacher, and friend to lover.

That is when *"hoary"* is *"glory!"*

In The Pages

Describe some of the characteristics of your favorite "hoary-headed" influences! Can you give thanks to God for what those people have done for you?

I Rebuke You!

October 17
Proverbs 17

"A rebuke goes deeper into one who has understanding than a hundred blows into a fool." Proverbs 17:10, NASB

"I solemnly charge you in the presence of God and of Christ Jesus, who is to judge the living and the dead, and by His appearing and His kingdom: preach the word; be ready in season and out of season; reprove, rebuke, exhort, with great patience and instruction." 2 Timothy 4:1-2, NASB

The older apostle (Paul) is reminding the young pastor (Timothy), the one left with the responsibility to steward the sheep, that he has duties in alignment with his authority. Part of that duty is to *rebuke*.

Trust me, the idea is as offensive to the pastor as it is the sheep. Real pastors, the ones with the gift (not just a title or position), will go there. But it's motivated by love and nurture for the sheep, not by some kind of control or image issue.

Pastors know that a little leaven can infect an entire lump of dough, so some may be quick to bring correction. But Paul adds that it must be *"with great patience and instruction."* That's what makes it proper governance. It requires the pastor to get his heart right prior to the rebuke.

The goal in mind is a change that benefits the one being rebuked, not the other way around. There is a little something here for all parties involved.

Solomon says the **gᵉʻârâh** (pronounced *gheh-aw-raw'*), or *"rebuke,"* comes packaged as *"reproof, reprimand, and/or criticism."* In this light, it makes it sound like it all depends on how the "receiver" handles it. It feels caustic and abrasive. Truth be told, most rebukes are.

It requires quite a bit of character on the receiving end to actually hear the truth of the message, regardless of how it was delivered. Wisdom says the person of *"understanding,"* defined in Hebrew as *"wise, discerning, intelligent, perceptive and teachable,"* receives the rebuke as helpful and sees another opportunity to make positive change. That says a lot about that person!

Whatever the action that prompted the correction in the first place, it's just a temporary blip on the radar—especially for the kind of person who receives a rebuke this well. The unique quality of receiving corrective feedback is a great indicator of what is happening deep inside of a person's character.

In classic proverbial contrast, the fool never allows the admonishment inside. It's all surface, and help rarely seeps below the bruise or external wound.

The Law allowed forty lashes. A hundred lashes is overkill; there's no use trying to help someone who can't be helped. That says quite a bit about the kind of prison a *"fool"* lives in. He can't get out, and no one gets in.

There's nothing healthy about that kind of place. The Body of Christ must live free of those kinds of restrictions!

In The Pages

Can you take a rebuke? Can you process a rebuke without taking rejection or offense? Will you apply the rebuke for real change? Can you give a rebuke in real love? Can you correct without too many demands for their change?

Big Honkin' Gifts

October 18
Proverbs 18

"A man's gift makes room for him, and brings him before great men." Proverbs 18:16, NKJV

"A gift gets attention; it buys the attention of eminent people." Proverbs 18:16, MSG

There are a number of different ways people interpret this verse. Most of us assume the *"gift"* is a bribe. But there really isn't any evidence whatsoever to support that kind of thinking. It is what it is, a simple truth that can be spiritual or natural in context.

We like gifts—wrapped or unwrapped, big or small, deserved or not. We like to be rewarded. The fact that someone took the time to give us a gift gets our attention. That is all this verse is saying. The *gift makes room* and opens doors.

The church is fairly infatuated with *gifts*. We like the BIG gifts, the "most important" gifts. You know what I'm talking about: the senior pastor, the healing evangelist, the big conference speaker with several published books, the wild-eyed prophet, even the self-proclaimed apostle, all usually carry the *gifts* we want, desire, and respect.

In our minds' eyes, those *"gifts"* are what got them to where they are. I'm not smiling as I write this. This is the biggest bunch of hooey the church has ever swallowed!

**Those *"gifts"* exist for the benefit of the Body,
not just the one stewarding the gift.**

28

The more serious question is this: what is more important, the gift or the character of the one who stewards the gift? Are the persons themselves a *gift* to you? Do you trust these people? Would you desire your children to learn from their ways and their tendencies?

Can you trust them with your spouse's wounds? Do you trust that their messages of covenant are not covertly steering your support, your money, your family, or ministry away from your life? Are they "within reach," or have they gotten so big that no one really has access to them?

Honestly, we are all partly responsible for this over-cooked stardom we project onto our religious leaders.

I'm not trying to be pissy about this. I just want us to rethink our obsession with the whole BIG *gifts* thing. "Big-giftedness" does not necessarily mean good character, integrity, or spiritual health.

So let me be clear. Real clear. Crystal clear: YOU ARE A GIFT!

That is, if you want to be. There is purpose for your life and a way for you to relate to the people and situations around you that makes a difference for the Kingdom! You are a *gift*, and God wants to make a way for you to touch and influence people.

Stop with the stargazing and being enamored with someone else's spiritual dealings. Get busy giving away what you have! I promise, you'll be fulfilled and greatly increased in your faithful use of what God has already given you!

Remember, big platforms and crowds don't automatically mean big productivity in the Kingdom. Read 1 Corinthians 1:26-28. *"God has chosen..."*

In The Pages

See Matthew 6:5. What is this saying about the traps of public recognition and applause in big-time ministry? Does God swoon over our gifts? Do you covet big gifts? What does 1 Peter 4:10 say about this topic?

Blame Game

October 19
Proverbs 19

"The foolishness of man ruins his way, and his heart rages against the Lord." Proverbs 19:3, NASB

"They will pass through the land hard-pressed and famished, and it will turn out that when they are hungry, they will be enraged and curse their king and their God as they face upward. Then they will look to the earth, and behold, distress and darkness, the gloom of anguish; and they will be driven away into darkness." Isaiah 8:21-22, NASB

I often wonder if the theme of Proverbs should be:

Stop blaming God for ALL your problems, and take a look in the mirror.

Seriously, most of the counsel tells us to consider our ways, change our minds, and examine our hearts. Crappy decisions yield crappy results.

We laugh and roll our eyes when we hear the overused Tony Robbins quote, *"If you do what you've always done, you'll get what you've always gotten."* But let's face it; recycling our ways while expecting different results is senseless.

I sincerely believe that Proverbs is coming from a place of a father's love, not a place of frustration. Dad sees through all of life's confusion, and with brilliant clarity, he reminds us that the *"foolishness of man"* is what's causing all of the ruckus down here, not God.

The NASB uses the word *"ruins."* The Hebrew word is **çâlaph** (pronounced *saw-laf*) meaning, *"to wrench or twist."* The fool is relentless in achieving his or her own way.

This translation is a bit more disruptive to our spirit, because it suggests that our *foolishness* undermines all authority and self-governance in order to achieve a less-than-positive outcome. Then, as the consequences of our actions begin to manifest, the "blame game" begins. We've seen it too many times.

Obviously, God (or God's earthly agent) is an easy target. You know what I'm talking about. People shouting, shaking their fists at what God did or didn't do? The people who act like this are people who have only heard about God, not the people who really know Him.

You would have to go back and read all of Isaiah 8 to get the full picture. But let me give you the skinny version. Israel and Judah were on the brink of being invaded by Assyria. The prophet Isaiah was encouraging them not to fear, but to bolster their resolve in the deliverance of God.

Chapter 9 even boasts of the promise—the coming of the Messiah. So swallow the gloom and anguish, and prepare to see God move! Israel was generally slow to receive a just word. So in total rebellion to what they knew and understood to be acceptable to God, they sought other sources of information for direction.

"When they say to you, 'Consult the mediums and the spiritists who whisper and mutter,' should not a people consult their God? Should they consult the dead on behalf of the living?" (Isaiah 8:19, NASB).

God takes this stuff personally. But this is on the people, not God. Sometimes God's people act like they've never known Him, His voice, or His desires . . . AT ALL.

Blame is easy, but it rarely fixes anything.

In The Pages

How prone are you to thinking that God is responsible for your hardships and pain? Have you ever said, "God, why did you let this happen?" Did He respond? Do you think God is responsible for everything hard? How much of your involvement do you equate to your struggles? When does blame fix anything?

Grapes

October 20
Proverbs 20

"Even a young man is known by his actions, whether his activity is pure and whether it is right." Proverbs 20:11, NET

"You will know them by their fruits. Grapes are not gathered from thorn bushes nor figs from thistles, are they?" Matthew 7:16, NASB

It may seem like a stretch to reference this verse from Matthew in regards to today's Proverb. Jesus was talking specifically about how to spot false prophets. But the principle still holds true, so we'll roll with it.

The Body just loves to use this verse to validate and measure the authenticity of another person's relationship with the Lord. But again, Jesus is discussing gates here, narrow ways—the people's declarations of *"Lord, Lord,"* (Matthew 7:21-23). My point:

> **External actions don't always tell us the whole truth about internal realities... ESPECIALLY in religious context.**

Honestly, it makes me nervous when religious church folk make judgments about another person's walk with God, based upon their own religious paradigms inside of their own church systems.

In relation to today's Proverb, we do need to be able to see some kind of *action*, or fruit, in order to make some assessments about development, especially with youth. Discipline and trained behavior is good and necessary. It is okay that some responses are based solely on etiquette, manners, and prior training.

Obviously, it's better when those responses stem from genuine honor, love, and respect. But you have to start somewhere, so discipline is good and helpful when encouraging young men and women, boys and girls, even children, to begin their journeys into maturity.

If Solomon is correct (and I believe he is), what is the best way to measure the weight of someone's *action*? The obvious answer is discipline. But what's behind that discipline?

There probably isn't a short answer, so let's just assume unconditional love really does work best for everyone. With children, discipline might include occasional punishment, but instruction out of a loving relationship is what's key. It's no different for us older folk.

I started very early with spiritual disciplines like devotionals, journaling, studying the Bible, prayer, and worship. And all of it has benefited me tremendously! I did them out of habit early on, and now, after many years of repetition, it is just a part of who I am. There is no dread, no boredom, and no internal pushback. It just happens, and it still feeds and blesses my soul.

It is during those "quiet times" that God works on my internal character issues, which is the whole point. Usually, I feel His nearness and gentle coaxing in my self-imposed disciplines, and that gives me greater access to The Voice that encourages me to act and be different.

In The Pages

How much of "how you are known" is due to discipline in your life? Do you see that as good, bad, or ugly? Explain.

Lazy Slugs

October 21
Proverbs 21

"The desire of the lazy man kills him, for his hands refuse to labor. He covets greedily all day long, but the righteous gives and does not spare." Proverbs 21:25-26, NKJV

"He who steals must steal no longer; but rather he must labor, performing with his own hands what is good, so that he will have something to share with one who has need." Ephesians 4:28, NASB

The subject of today's lesson is about the *"lazy man."* In 2 Thessalonians 3:10, Paul tells the church that a person who has no plans to work should have no plans to eat. Solomon's use of the Hebrew word **'âtsêl** (pronounced *aw-tsale'*), translated in the NASB as *"sluggard,"* and in the NKJV as *"lazy man,"* is exclusive to Proverbs and holds broad moral implications.

It's more than just laziness we're talking about here, at least in the way we usually think of laziness. Proverbs compares the *sluggard* to being unstable and apathetic. Solomon describes him as irresponsible, without governance and stewardship.

If the absence of moral character is the problem, then we can expect less-than-favorable tactics from these people when it comes to meeting their own needs and desires. In today's verse from Ephesians, Paul reprimands and tells the thief to get a bona fide job and earn a righteous wage. If you're unwilling to do that, you are stealing blessing from yourself.

We all know that a person in *greed* rarely responds properly to the needs around him. His scarcity-mindset will always argue with him that there won't be enough left for him if he gives away what he has.

I love the fact that Paul points out in today's text that one of the biggest blessings of work is that it gives a person the opportunity to sow blessing into the lives of those with need. This is true spiritual giving!

Giving under compulsion, or because you think God is going to be disappointed in you if you do not give, is to miss the heart of God. Paul has already done the math. We are the ones blessed the most by sharing what we have!

Earlier in his letter to the Ephesians, Paul writes,

"In Him we have redemption through His blood, the forgiveness of our trespasses, according to the riches of His grace which He lavished on us. In all wisdom and insight..." (Ephesians 1:7-8, NASB).

The word I want us to catch here is *"lavished."* It means *"super-excessive, super-abounding, super-above, and over the top!"* In short, Jesus did the work so He could give to us freely, abundantly, all with super-generosity!

This is the example we are supposed to live by.

Jesus said, *"And as you go, preach, saying, 'The kingdom of heaven is at hand.' Heal the sick, raise the dead, cleanse the lepers, cast out demons. Freely you received, freely give"* (Matthew 10:7-8, NASB).

This is when we can be at our best! When we are fully aware of all that God has done for us, and out of that awareness flows a gracious heart that can't help but be *lavish* with what we give to those who have need! This is Kingdom living!

In The Pages

I have often taught, *"Christians have a greater need to give, than the poor has to receive."* What do you think that means? Do you think modern Christians are automatically generous? Why or why not?

Common Bond

October 22
Proverbs 22

"The rich and the poor have a common bond, the Lord is the maker of them all." Proverbs 22:2, NASB

"Therefore, listen to me, you men of understanding. Far be it from God to do wickedness, and from the Almighty to do wrong [. . .] Who shows no partiality to princes nor regards the rich above the poor, for they all are the work of His hands? In a moment they die, and at midnight people are shaken and pass away, and the mighty are taken away without a hand. For His eyes are upon the ways of a man, and He sees all his steps." Job 34:10, 19-21, NASB

The Hebrew suggests that this *"common bond"* is all part of His master plan to force interdependence among humanity. Our God is a relational God. He has designed us for personal connection and intertwined involvement, despite all the excuses we use to separate ourselves.

The strict meaning of **pâgash** (pronounced *paw-gash´*) stipulates a coming together, either by accident or aggressive purpose.

God is not partial. He does not show preference. He doesn't love the rich more than He loves the poor. He doesn't sit and calculate whom He wants to bless and whom He doesn't. He doesn't have favorites.

He doesn't formulate elite clubs and societies. He doesn't favor one race or tribe over another. He doesn't pick and choose who gets saved and who doesn't. All of that is in the hands of man.

"*For there is no partiality with God*" (Romans 2:11, NASB).

"*For God does not show favoritism*" (Romans 2:11, NIV).

To summarize what the Apostle Paul was talking about during this very intense discussion, mankind has more to do with mankind's conditions and directions than the predetermined prejudice of God.

The one thing we can be absolutely certain of *has* been predetermined and sealed is His relentless and thorough love. He loves us all greatly and completely. **GOD IS LOVE** (1 John 4:16).

A lot of people question, and even vehemently reject, this idea because of hardships they have suffered. It's hard to see God as loving and fair if you feel like He kicks the figgy pudding out of you on a regular basis.

If you were abused or rejected by the people who were supposed to protect you and love you unconditionally, then you might struggle with the concept that

God does not play favorites. It's understandable how something like that could make you say, *"Show me the love of God! Where is it?"*

We all get sidetracked from time to time with frustration with hardship and unanswered questions. It's during those times that we need to really lean on each other, regardless of our differences.

We need a tangible show of love, to give away and to receive. We need each other, in a *common bond* with friend and stranger, to give each other hope and encouragement and to remind one another that God does loves us!

In The Pages

Have you ever felt like God was picking on you or was singling you out for hardship or punishment? How do you find peace when those kinds of thoughts come? Why do you think people are quicker to believe God is angry with them, than to trust in His great ability to forgive and bless?

Chasing Bank

October 23
Proverbs 23

"Don't wear yourself out trying to get rich; restrain yourself! Riches disappear in the blink of an eye; wealth sprouts wings and flies off into the wild blue yonder." Proverbs 23:4-5, MSG

Money is not a bad thing. There is no question that men and women of unique talents and generous hearts have sown large sums of money into countless philanthropic and charity-based operations worldwide! Most church and parachurch ministries exist and operate solely due to the donations of their supporters.

You may have heard of something called the "Joseph Anointing." A Joseph is one who is a provider both spiritually and materially for those in the Body of Christ. It is a person who understands that he is simply the manager of all that God has entrusted to him.

In today's church, "Josephs" are usually businessmen who get Kingdom concepts and actually carry a supernatural ability to make money solely to fund and support ministry projects.

We're not watering down today's scripture by acknowledging the legitimacy of financial abundance and the need for spiritually sensitive stewards who have hearts to fund and support projects all over the planet! It takes money to evangelize, to send out missionaries, to dig wells, to feed orphans, to build schools, and to clothe the poor. It takes bank!

What today's text is cautioning is an obsession with trying to get personally rich. There is nothing in scripture that points to Joseph ever having a desire to be rich. I doubt he had his sights set on being number two in Egypt either. His dream was telling, but not specific.

No doubt, Joseph was anointed! But that anointing and favor followed him through good times and bad times. Some people seem to have this unique ability to make money without really even trying. Whatever they are dabbling in works, and it works well.

Having reasonable portfolio goals is one thing. Being driven with an all-consuming lust for wealth, is quite another. It may not be the best way to spend one's life energy.

"Do not store up for yourselves treasures on earth, where moth and rust destroy, and where thieves break in and steal. But store up for yourselves treasures in heaven, where neither moth nor rust destroys, and where thieves do not break in or steal; for where your treasure is, there your heart will be also" (Matthew 6:19-21, NASB).

God doesn't have a problem with rich people. That's not what Jesus is getting at here. He's saying that security comes through relationship with God, not from our bank accounts!

Whatever you have here on earth, none of it spends as eternal currency! It's not a bad thing if you've done well for yourself, financially. Just be careful that it does not possess you.

In The Pages

Read 1 Timothy 6:6-12 and Hebrews 13:5-6. What lessons can we glean from these teachings by the Apostle Paul? What kind of problems do you think wealthy people face with their material possessions? How can you apply Luke 12:48 to today's topic?

Clout

October 24
Proverbs 24

"Do not lie in wait like an outlaw against a righteous man's house, do not raid his dwelling place; for though a righteous man falls seven times, he rises again, but the wicked are brought down by calamity." Proverbs 24:15-16, NIV

HERE IN YOUR PRESENCE
Jon Egan © Vertical Worship Songs. Used by permission.[4]

Found in Your hands, fullness of joy
Every fear suddenly wiped away
Here in Your presence
All of my gains now fade away
Every crown no longer on display
Here in Your presence
Heaven is trembling in awe of Your wonders
The kings and their kingdoms are standing amazed

The wise King is making an incredibly prophetic statement. If you tend to lean towards less-than-admirable tactics, it is in your best interest NOT to mess with a *righteous man*.

That man lives with the conviction that God is with him, and for him. Even if he *falls seven times* (which implies an indefinite number), you can expect God to pick him right back up!

On the other hand, wickedness does not pay long-term benefits. Sooner or later, we'll pay for our dances with darkness. A *righteous man* finds himself in the arms of a loving God, no matter what swirls around him. Even joy manifests while the devil laughs.

Such confidence of the *righteous* comes from the deeper place of rest inside his or her heart! What peace the King speaks today!

In the early days, the apostles were kicking some butt in Jerusalem. The people were being healed, just by being in the shadow of Peter (Acts 5:15). Signs and wonders were as common as street vendors, and evangelism and demonic deliverance flowed like wine in Napa!

Of course, the High Priest and the Sadducees were enraged with jealousy. If this stuff continued, they would be out of a job! Their reputations were on the line. When all you have is dead religion, this kind of wonderment makes the ordinary look impotent and irrelevant. Hence, the rage and jealousy!

The legalistic sect tried to imprison the apostolic troublemakers (Acts 5:17-18), but angels kept interrupting their plans (Acts 5:19-20). So they convened a meeting to strategize how to have them killed (Acts 5:33).

When the boys were out in the streets the next day, doing their thing, the council had them arrested again and brought in for questioning. After a very moving testimony by Peter, the councilors were all *cut to the quick* by this piercing truth and scratching conviction! Shouts of death and murder arose, and it wasn't looking too good for Jesus' apostles.

Suddenly, Wisdom spoke.

> *"Men of Israel, take care what you propose to do with these men"* (Acts 5:35, NASB).

Gamaliel had enough sense to see they were in over their heads, and they might be striking the heels of *righteous men,* who had God clout. He reminded them that to attack men and women who really walk with God is a personal attack on God (Acts 5:38-39). Smart guy.

In The Pages

Is this promise only for apostles or church leaders? Do you walk in this kind of confidence about yourself, your family, or your friends?

Search It Out

October 25
Proverbs 25

"It is the glory of God to conceal a matter, but the glory of kings is to search out a matter." Proverbs 25:2, NASB

For way too many years, I believed the only way God speaks is through the Bible. I'm not sure how I arrived at such a conclusion, but I did.

I had a bunch of other crazy notions that totally ignored the work of the Holy Spirit and all the other relational attributes of a living God. Once I discovered the personal nature of the Holy Spirit, God began to unravel my theological hardwiring. I was like Alice who fell through the rabbit's hole.

God was speaking everywhere, in ways that were almost too wonderful to comprehend! I wanted to sample everything on the Lord's buffet. I didn't have to rationalize away the voice of God anymore. The gifts of the Spirit were real and applicable in the most magnificent, yet simply tangible ways.

No longer did I have to proof-text life through the scriptures. As I removed the preset boundaries of my God experience (as determined only by the Holy Writ), I was propelled into a deeper faith and trust in hearing the voice of God in the most unusual ways.

I wonder if Moses would have still felt led to confront Pharaoh, simply by reading the Torah?

Would Peter have come to the same conclusions about the Gentiles without the supernatural voice of God?

Would Mary have remained peaceful about her growing belly without a visitation from heaven?

Would Joseph have tolerated his betrothed's holy expansion without a clear message in a night vision?

One more, would David have seen his sin concerning Bathsheba's husband without a direct word from God via the prophet Nathan?

In all sincerity, I seriously doubt that reading the Bible alone would have produced the same results.

It was all about hearing God's voice.

Part of interpreting dreams has to do with our *searching out a matter*. We rarely pay attention to our dreams because we assume last night's pizza is what caused that pink monkey to drive that minivan into our neighbor's swimming pool!

But sometimes God gives us these bizarre dreams that require us to use natural discipline to search out what God is saying to us! Check this out:

"Indeed God speaks once, or twice, yet no one notices it. In a dream, a vision of the night, when sound sleep falls on men, while they slumber in their beds, then He opens the ears of men, and seals their instruction, that He may turn

man aside from his conduct, and keep man from pride; He keeps back his soul from the pit, and his life from passing over into Sheol" (Job 33:14-18, NASB).

The bottom line here is that God is still creatively communicating.

The bigger question is, are we willing to *search out* all the ways in which He communicates? We are royalty in His Kingdom! We each have a duty to hear and obey; no matter what method He uses to get our attention. My fellow kings and queens... search it out!

In The Pages

What do you do with your dreams? I highly recommend the book, *Understanding the Dreams you Dream*, by Ira Milligan.[5]

Friendly Fire

October 26
Proverbs 26

"Like an archer who wounds at random is he who hires a fool or any passer-by." Proverbs 26:10, NIV

Wikipedia defines "friendly fire" as *"inadvertent firing towards one's own or otherwise friendly forces while attempting to engage enemy forces, particularly where this results in injury or death."*

It happens too often in war. The numbers are staggering. There were a reported 8,000 incidents in the Vietnam War alone.

The numbers from WWI and WWII are equally disturbing. Poor communication and bad weather resulted in total chaos and disorder in Normandy. Airborne divisions, who dropped behind enemy lines prior to the bombings, were scattered all over the place. And some found themselves in areas where bombs were finding their targets.

One of the most heart-wrenching scenes in the movie *Braveheart* is when England's cowardly King Edward Longshanks orders his archers to intentionally fire into a mass of Scottish and English warriors who were engaged in hand-to-hand combat. Obviously, it was a total disregard for the welfare of his men, so it doesn't really qualify as "friendly fire," but more in the realm of fratricide. With all that said, this is what I believe today's text is talking about.

Solomon is warning us that we need to have some discernment when it comes to choosing the people we partner with in our life affairs. The text refers specifically to an employer, but it's sound wisdom for all of us.

The fact that the warning is against hiring a careless drunk suggests that ignoring this warning is like inviting friendly fire to be released in your own perimeters. It is sound tutelage, and all this talk of weaponry and mishaps is a little alarming.

It is a sensible notion to think about what potential damage could happen to those around us. An irresponsible fool with the keys to a weapons cache is definitely sketchy. But I wonder if there is something more commonplace in regards to friendly fire we should be aware of all around us—the Body of Christ.

"...but through love serve one another. For the whole Law is fulfilled in one word, in the statement, 'You shall love your neighbor as yourself.' But if you bite and devour one another, take care that you are not consumed by one another" (Galatians 5:13-15, NASB).

Friendly fire happens among God's children. The Greek word **katĕsthiŏ** (pronounced *kat-es-thee'-o*) means, *"to eat or nibble down."*

Gossip, slander, jealousy, and division, all provide opportunity for gross wounding and invite the presence of the *accuser of the brethren* (Revelations 12:10), who wildly applauds as we bite each other!

Do we really want that scumbag involved in our business?

The anti-venom is humility, preference, submission to each other, honor, selfless service, and of course, unconditional love. I've often heard that the church is about the only institution that shoots its wounded. There is no bright future in firing upon our own brothers and sisters!

In The Pages

What does Galatians 5:16-18 recommend for avoiding friendly fire? Continue reading verses 19-21. What other problems are evident in the church's ground war with darkness and selfish saints?

Jealous

October 27
Proverbs 27

"Wrath is fierce and anger is a flood, but who can stand before jealousy?" Proverbs 27:4, NASB

"But if you have bitter jealousy and selfish ambition in your heart, do not be arrogant and so lie against the truth. This wisdom is not that which comes down from above, but is earthly, natural, demonic. For where jealousy and selfish ambition exist, there is disorder and every evil thing." James 3:14-16, NASB

This is nasty business here. Solomon reflects on the fact that we can be downright cruel when we are basting in our own poisonous *anger* or rage-filled indignation.

That kind of *anger* can swell like the Mississippi during flood season. It might be contained for a short while, but continued rain soon has it spilling over the levee, free to do its destructive damage.

To be fair, there are times when emotions explode in a moment, or for a season, and then subside as quickly as they arose. This is not the way it happens with *jealousy*. The waters don't subside, the destruction is not repaired, and the flood continues to destroy until there is nothing left.

We've seen it on the news countless times. A *jealous* husband kills his wife. A *jealous* wife murders her husband's mistress. And then these people take their own lives. Absolutely tragic! Pastor James says this kind of merciless revenge is driven by the demonic influences of hell (James 3:15).

The Hebrew word for *"jealous"* is **qin'âh** (pronounced *kin-aw'*), which means *"zealous envy."* The Greek gives us a little more insight. The word is **zēlŏs** (pronounced *dzay'-los*) also meaning, *"zeal,"* but it's a zeal that is often planted deep and often recycles itself repeatedly in the minds of the offended.

There is no end to those feelings of rejection or the hurt from those wounds. It regenerates over and over, driving that person mad, until the voices of darkness take over, giving all sorts of suggestions as to how to rectify the situation.

Don't confuse covetness with *jealousy*. To *"covet"* means to see something you want and are motivated to go after, like when David saw Bathsheba in her birthday suit. This can be a big problem when it's something you're not supposed to have, or it's not yours to take.

Jealousy is when someone else has something you want (or maybe something you don't want), and it eats away at you that they have it. For example, let's say I lead a Bible study group that I love and cherish. But I see that my friend leads a much bigger Bible study. Even though I know that many people would be too much for me to manage, I still hate the fact that my friend has that group. If I can't manage a group that size, why should he get to? I hate his success. That's what it means to fall prey to *jealousy*!

That kind of thinking would motivate me to manifest a hellish attitude and either slander my friend or discredit his group, for whatever reason the devil suggests. It's nasty business, people!

Extreme cases can end violently. *"Cain rose up against his brother and killed him"* (Genesis 4:8, NASB).

Unfortunately, this is a fairly common generational sin. It gets passed down the bloodline. If this is something you struggle with, it's time to cut some soul ties and get out of that cycle!

Jealousy will make your life a living hell.

In The Pages

Most of our problems begin with "me." Do you agree with that? Why or why not? If you struggle with jealousy, what rejected you? Who denied you? What offended you? Have you asked for help, prayer, or a listening ear for confession?

Behind the Curtain

October 28
Proverbs 28

"Better is the poor that walketh in his uprightness, than he that is perverse in his ways, though he be rich." Proverbs 28:6, KJV

Less than a week ago, we discussed how God does not show partiality when it comes to wealth. He doesn't make certain people wealthy because He loves them more. He doesn't use poverty to punish others. We have much more to do with all of that than He does.

Today's scripture reminds us that God cares much more about our *"uprightness"* (our integrity) than He does about us having money. One of the commentaries I consult regularly (The NET Bible) says, *"honest poverty is better than corrupt wealth."* Honesty is better than corruption. Period.

"The fear of the Lord is clean, enduring forever; the judgments of the Lord are true; they are righteous altogether. They are more desirable than gold, yes, than much fine gold; sweeter also than honey and the drippings of the honeycomb" (Psalms 19:9-10, NASB).

David is saying that God's presence in our lives is worth far more than any measure of material goods. He says the *beginning of knowledge and wisdom*, which is the *"fear of the Lord"* (Proverbs 1:7), is clean, pure, and fair.

There is a blessing for the one who lives in integrity. A life that is clean produces pure satisfaction that grafts enjoyment in the simplest of life's pleasures. It doesn't take financial security to be at peace and live graciously. Integrity and character are the most *desirable* and enduring qualities of all.

Today's Proverb challenges our ways, our walks, our responses to what life hands us. The people around us can help support us on our pursuits of integrity.

A vested community should demand our very best; yet still offer forgiveness when we give less than what is required.

But what about the stuff no one else sees?

Early on in my spiritual development, a dear brother complimented me on how well I performed externally around the religious community. But then he said,

> *"But who you really are is what manifests when no one is watching... when you are behind the curtain."*

His eyes were piercing, nearly burning a hole right through me. It was a very uncomfortable moment. But I knew what he was saying was right on. It was haunting; because it dawned on me that this is exactly the truth with God. God sees beyond all the external stuff. He sees our inner mechanisms, our thoughts—our hidden lives. It's a sobering reminder to walk in *uprightness*!

In The Pages

How good do you feel about your "when no one is watching" life? When was the last time you heard the Spirit lovingly say, "Do you want to reconsider that decision?" Do you push back, or do you really try to listen to His counsel?

Hangman

October 29
Proverbs 29

"In the transgression of an evil person there is a snare, but a righteous person can sing and rejoice." Proverbs 29:6, NET

When I was a kid, I often heard my mom say, *"What goes around, comes around."* A buddy's dad would say it this way, *"That's the screwing you get for the screwing you got."*

Today's Proverb is saying the same thing. The *"snare,"* the trap, some kind of nasty little contraption, lays ready to pay back the one who set it in the first place.

There are both natural and spiritual consequences to blatant sin. We're all guilty of sin. But today's text is referring to the **ra'** (pronounced *rah*)—*"the person who is consumed with evil."*

The person who consistently chooses evil guarantees himself consistently bad returns. That's just the way it is.

There are many juicy plots in the Book of Esther. What a story! The way of living back then is so very foreign to our modern day culture, though the grace and elegance of Esther still warms our hearts! She was something else!

When I read today's Proverb, I immediately thought of the story of Haman and Mordecai. If you haven't read the entire story, do yourself a favor and give it a whirl! I have yet to read a novel with this much drama! For sake of space, I'll give you the cliff notes:

Mordecai and his beautiful cousin, Esther (who he had taken in as his own daughter), were both Jews in a land full of deported Jews, under the control of the Persian King Xerxes. Esther eventually became Queen to Xerxes.

When Mordecai caught wind of a plot by the king's own men to remove Xerxes from the throne, Mordecai stepped in, foiling the plan. Mordecai was regularly seen at the king's gate among the king's officials, but he didn't participate in the pagan trappings of paying homage to the King.

Xerxes' right-hand man was Haman. He hated Mordecai and all the Jews. He petitioned Xerxes to rid the land of all of the Jews. But his hidden agenda was to have Mordecai hanged on gallows he had personally designed. The only problem was that Xerxes did not realize his approval of Haman's plan also meant death to Queen Esther.

After much prayer, fasting, and strategic planning, Esther made the bold decision to approach Xerxes on behalf of the Jews and reveal Haman's evil plot. King Xerxes was mortified to learn that Haman's plans included the death of his beloved wife!

"So they hanged Haman on the gallows which he had prepared for Mordecai, and the king's anger subsided" (Esther 7:10, NASB).

Go read the entire story! It's a great read, and a tremendous reminder that a person with evil character can expect snares, nooses, and self-inflicted harm. What goes around does come around.[6]

In The Pages

Do you have personal experience with laying traps for yourself? Was your mistake spontaneous or premeditated? Do the effects of payback still linger? How else would you articulate the truths in all of today's text?

Eagles

October 30
Proverbs 30

"The eye that mocks his father, and scorns obedience to his mother, the ravens of the valley will pick it out, and the young eagles will eat it." Proverbs 30:17, NKJV

Honoring and obeying parents is one of the more repetitive lessons in Proverbs. Today's verse paints a less-than-pretty picture.

I can only imagine the impact to a little six-year-old kid hearing this for the first time. Why not tell him trolls live under bridges and eat children who wander too far away from home? Same effect.

I'm sure Solomon had seen a battlefield or two, laden with bloated corpses in the boiling sun. Scavengers of the air would then circle, descend, and feed on the fallen. These kinds of gory images make an impression on anyone, regardless of age.

Several other Bible translations (NIV, NLT, RSV, NET) define the Hebrew word **nesher** (pronounced *neh'-sher*) as *"vulture"* instead of *"eagle."* This word is found about 30 times in the Old Testament and is consistently translated as *"eagle"* elsewhere.

My assumption is that the translators changed the word to vultures in this particular verse because *eagles* are not scavengers. They normally only feast on what they kill. Eagles are not attracted to carrion. They can be trained to eat what they haven't killed, but that isn't natural to them.

It makes sense to change the word to vulture based on the imagery described here, but as I've pointed out, that would be to go against how the word is consistently used throughout scripture. I think there is prophetic purpose in using the word *"eagles."* I want to ask you to push out a bit with me prophetically, into the haze, and let's see if the Spirit has a confirmation waiting to ignite hope in our hearts.

Could it be that Solomon is saying that the *"young eagles"* (who are a picture of those with keen eyesight, insight, and the ability to soar high above the terrains of earth) will capitalize and ingest the truths learned from the hardships that surface on this orb? They will glean from the mistakes of others.

The *"mockers"* and those full of *"scorn"* will forfeit their inheritances and suffer the fate that the scavengers deal them. But the *eagles* will profit. The *eagles* will learn. The *eagles* will benefit and capitalize on every opportunity to live true to their pure *eagle* nature!

Majesty and honor is the current of their soaring. Yes, the *eagles* will consume the rich morsels of character that others may toss aside, but they will quickly return to the heights where they were fashioned to live and exist.

"Yet those who wait for the Lord will gain new strength; they will mount up with wings like eagles, they will run and not get tired, they will walk and not become weary" (Isaiah 40:31, NASB).

The *young eagles* will do what *eagles* are supposed to do.

In The Pages

If there is any motivation in today's lesson, what is it? What is the call to your heart? Do you think there is more in this verse than just proper respect for parents? What else do you hear?

Hen House

October 31
Proverbs 31

"The words of King Lemuel, the utterance which his mother taught him: What, my son? And what, son of my womb? And what, son of my vows? Do not give your strength to women, nor your ways to that which destroys kings." Proverbs 31:1-3, NKJV

Now King Solomon loved many foreign women along with the daughter of Pharaoh: Moabite, Ammonite, Edomite, Sidonian, and Hittite women, from the nations concerning which the Lord had said to the sons of Israel, "You shall not associate with them, nor shall they associate with you, for they will surely turn your heart away after their gods." Solomon held fast to these in love. He had seven hundred wives, princesses, and three hundred concubines, and his wives turned his heart away. For when Solomon was old, his wives turned his heart away after other gods; and his heart was not wholly devoted to the Lord his God, as the heart of David his father had been." 1 Kings 11:1-4, NASB

We are not certain, but it's probable that King Lemuel was Solomon. If so, we should feel much more weight on momma's plea to her son.

Bathsheba had been through some stuff. She suffered the pain of a murdered husband and the loss of a child. I have often imagined what it would be like to sit down to tea and biscuits with Bathsheba and ask her if she knew exactly what she was doing when she laid down her robes and bathed nude within clear view of the King's deck?

Maybe such a thing was much more common in those days? One thing is for certain: once David saw her, it was over! She was swept up in a consensual whirlwind that brought much destruction. So I think she was motivated to warn her dear boy, to lovingly and passionately bring truth about living a life of seasoned honor.

She calls Solomon the *"son of my vows."* This tells me she had done some soul searching about how she and David had connected. They had paid dearly for their liaisons, and she had made promises in dedicating her son to the Lord!

God takes the course of a person's life very seriously, once that life has been dedicated to Him by the child's parents.

Solomon was anointed, no doubt, but he had quite an appetite for the ladies. I guess momma knew the apple wouldn't fall too far from the tree.

1 Kings 11 pretty much lays it out. Contrary to the wisdom his mother gave him, Solomon gave away his *"strength to women"* and also gave in to *"that which destroys kings."*

He gave away his **chayil** (pronounced *khah'-yil*), his honor, his strength, his valor, his power, his riches and ultimately his respect. The King became so caught up in his interest in the ladies (and the man had some women!) that he lost the respect, and ultimately the authority of his position, due to his forfeit of responsibilities.

His loss of focus in who had put him into authority resulted in the diminishment of what could have been the most glorious reign of a King in Israel's history! It all turned his heart from his God and his duties. The destruction was sadly predictable.

In The Pages

Who was the problem here, Solomon or his foreign wives? Can you make a case for the manifestation of generational sin (Exodus 34:6-7)? What validation do you see in your own lineage?

A Darker Kind of Blind

November 1
Proverbs 1

"Turn to my reproof, behold, I will pour out my spirit on you; I will make my words known to you." Proverbs 1:23 NASB

One of the saddest scenes in scripture is when Jesus says to the Pharisees,

"You search the Scriptures because you think that in them you have eternal life; it is these that testify about Me; and you are unwilling to come to Me so that you may have life" (John 5:39-40, NASB).

What Jesus is saying is that they have spent an entire lifetime searching the Scriptures for all their answers to life, only to have **THE** answer standing right in front of them, and they were too dull, too full of religious piety, and too spiritually insensitive to realize it.

These were devout men. They worked hard to uphold the law and do what they thought God wanted and commanded them to do. But somewhere along the way, they got lost. Everything they had asked for, prayed for, and believed for, was standing in front of their very eyes, and they simply could not see Him.

I wonder how many times I've missed Him in front of me too?

How many times have I given the proper biblical response, but not actually sought out God's spirit and counsel? How often have I been right in principle, but very wrong in my heart and attitude on how I handled a situation?

Wisdom tells us the Spirit of God is willing to make His secrets known to us, to give us understanding and insight. But there comes a point where we have to come into His presence in order to really acquire that knowledge.

The Holy Spirit always seems to know the way into my calloused heart. He can bring loving correction, or a stern rebuke, in any number of different ways. Whichever way He chooses to speak to me, it's always in a manner, which brings the greatest amplification of whatever truth I need in that moment.

"So, Mike, what is your point?"

I'm glad you asked. My point is that the technical truth of the text is not always enough. We need the seasoning of the Lord's presence, His voice, the Spirit, to help us apply what we've learned. Seasons change; people change. We need fresh and continuous revelation that is relevant, applicable, and appropriate. Otherwise, you're just going to be known as another religious zealot who checked his heart at the door.

In The Pages

When is the last time you grabbed your Bible to look for an answer? When is the last time you activated your faith by using your prayer language or praying with your mind? How much easier is all of that when combined with generous amounts of worship, both privately and corporately? What is your bottom-line thought about the help of the Holy Spirit when it comes to the application of truth?

Plan? What Plan?

November 2
Proverbs 2

"Discretion will protect you, and understanding will guard you." Proverbs 2:11, NASB

"Good Sense will scout ahead for danger, insight will keep an eye out for you." Proverbs 2:11, MSG

Context is everything when you're trying to understand why a writer says what he says. Proverbs 2 discusses how to pursue wisdom and the benefits of that pursuit. Today's text is more along the lines of the latter: **the benefits of protection and safeguards.**

In the Hebrew, there are several different variations for the word *"discretion"* in the Old Testament. The word used here today is **mᵉzimmâh** (pronounced **mez-im-maw'**), which implies *"a plan or intent."*

That word caught my attention today; because I know most serious-minded followers of Christ want to do what pleases the Lord. Unfortunately, too many of them are hung in suspense as they wait on the "perfect will of God." It's a very hot topic, especially around young believers.

I think a lot of that has to do with an unhealthy fear that God is not pleased with us, and we have to "get it right" in order to earn His love and affection (been there; done that). It's a whole lot of unnecessary sweat and stress.

God is love. No matter what mistakes we make or how it turns out, none of it warrants more or less love from Him. He accepts and approves of us. So can we stop begging God to direct every little step we take?

The protection piece is real inside of wisdom. A plan is good. What plan, you ask?

A plan to pursue God.

A plan to praise and worship Him regardless of how you feel.

A plan to love anyone and everyone.

A plan to be a giver, and not just a taker.

A plan to prefer those around us.

A plan to die to some of our hyper-sensitive awareness of what "I" need.

A plan to see the need of "others" around us, and respond accordingly.

A plan to pray in order to reactivate my faith and awareness of God's presence... even when my circumstances suck.

A plan isn't always about direction. Sometimes a plan is nothing more than premeditated exercise of our will for our own preservation and strength.

Spiritual defaults that heighten our awareness that God is with me, on me, and around me! You'll be surprised as to what kind of target that gives the Holy Spirit to land on!

The *parakalete* (the Holy Spirit) is the one who puts His back to your back, with sword drawn! So there is real comfort and protection in our walks to Him. Wisdom expects that response every time!

In The Pages

Where do you default when you get stuck? Let me say it another way: how do you medicate when you are hurting? Would it help you to have a plan about the direction you'll go before you find yourself in the next pit? What will your plan be when the wheels fall off (they do that every now and then, you know)?

Golf Clap

November 3
Proverbs 3

"Don't lose your grip on Love and Loyalty. Tie them around your neck; carve their initials on your heart. Earn a reputation for living well in God's eyes and the eyes of the people." Proverbs 3:3-4, MSG

This is seriously beautiful counsel. Eugene Peterson has made it about as clear as you can make it. The New American Standard uses the word *"kindness"* in the place of *"love."*

*"Do not let **kindness** and truth leave you; bind them around your neck, write them on the tablet of your heart. So you will find favor and good repute in the sight of God and man"* (Proverbs 3:3-4, NASB).

"Kindness" is probably the proper word to use linguistically, but *"love"* really gets the point across. We've touched on this the past couple of days. It's not just about speaking truth. It's *how* we share truth and how we live out the message of the gospel. It has to be rooted in love, especially when we're "out there" in the dirty and not safe inside the walls of the church.

We know that *kindness* is one of the fruits of the Spirit. But that kindness has to come out of a pure heart. We shouldn't act "kindly" to others for the mere hope of receiving a "golf clap" from Heaven. Religious works rarely get the applause of mankind in general, nor does God recognize those works.

Religious people notice religious activity.

That's who you'll get your "golf clap" from.

So, what does it take to gain favor in God's eyes?

"My counsel is this: Live freely, animated and motivated by God's Spirit. Then you won't feed the compulsions of selfishness. For there is a root of sinful self-interest in us that is at odds with a free spirit, just as the free spirit is incompatible with selfishness. These two ways of life are antithetical, so that you cannot live at times one way and at times another way according to how

you feel on any given day. Why don't you choose to be led by the Spirit and so escape the erratic compulsions of a law-dominated existence" (Galatians 5:16-18, MSG).

True freedom allows us to respond to people with the kind of love and kindness Proverbs is talking about today, because that's what is inside of us. There isn't pressure to be a certain way because we fear God's wrath.

Wisdom would have us moving with an openness and genuine desire to embrace what and whom we are around. When our response, which flows from our heart and spirit, produces the Lord's kindness and ease of access, people will notice and respond.

Although it's not the goal, it will turn heads . . . because He has shown up!

In The Pages

Are you kind and gentle with people, or does your spirit fruit fluctuate with your moods? Today's Galatians passage seems to suggest that selfishness and self-interest is a direct attack upon your real freedom. How do you suppose this is true?

DOA

November 4
Proverbs 4

"The way of the wicked is like darkness; they do not know over what they stumble." Proverbs 4:19, NASB

"Jesus answered, 'Are there not twelve hours in the day? If anyone walks in the day, he does not stumble, because he sees the light of this world. But if one walks in the night, he stumbles, because the light is not in him'." John 11:9-10, NKJV

Many years ago, I accompanied my buddy, Evangelist Isaiah Reed[7], to a meeting in Victoria, Texas. It was a very cool little Hispanic church that had actually taken over and cleaned up a prior "gentlemen's" club. Cool indeed.

We had finished worship, and Isaiah was telling his story. He had gotten to the part where a Columbian drug dealer had shot him in the head (twice) and stabbed him 16 times in his neck, shoulders, and back! (I've seen the scars; I know the story is legit.) Isaiah was then thrown from the car in the middle of downtown Denver. He said, *"All my years as a pimp and drug dealer were flashing before me. I'm laying there, in the street, in my own blood, not able to really comprehend that this is how my life is going to end."*

Then he said, *"About that time, sound went away, and I could see that all light was disappearing from in front of me. Darkness came for me."* As he's telling this part, every light in that little church suddenly went out. People started to panic. It was pitch black!

I was on the front row. I yelled as loud as I could, *"Use it, Isaiah! Finish the story!"* From that point on, it was masterful!

In that darkness, Isaiah spoke of a darkness that is beyond the void of light. He saw darkness, he felt darkness, and he eventually succumbed to that darkness. He died on that cold asphalt, all alone. When the ambulance arrived, he was pronounced DOA (dead on arrival).

I could leave you hanging, but that would be mean.

The man was actually brought back to life by the prayers of his momma as she prophesied to him while he lay dead in the hospital morgue.

Time and space won't allow me to give you all the details. It's your choice whether or not you choose to believe. But this story is supernatural and miraculous!

The stranger truth is that Isaiah didn't turn his life over to the Lord immediately after that. He went back to pimping and drugs for another three years. So God came again, in another way, and sealed the deal for a total heart and life change. Isaiah and his wife (one of his ex-call girls) have been a fire-breathing soul-winning team ever since! It is quite the story of God's unfathomable mercy!

The point here is that Wisdom implores us to not make it that hard! There is another way to live. Invite the light. Invite the presence of the Holy Spirit to illuminate your mind and your ways.

Stumbling happens, either because you're not paying attention or because you can't see. Let your light shine!

In The Pages

Most of our own personal deliverance has much to do with our courage to pull what is in the dark into light. How encouraged are you with that process right now in your life? If you had to name something you know needs to come to light, but you were not ready to deal with it today, what would it be? What is better than freedom?

Bad Honey

November 5
Proverbs 5

"For the lips of an adulteress drip honey and smoother than oil is her speech." Proverbs 5:3, NASB

There is a "but" at the beginning of the next verse that is horrifying: *"**But** in the end she is bitter as wormwood, sharp as a two-edged sword"* (Proverbs 5:4, NASB).

Hang with it for a couple more verses and let the reality of those possibilities sink deep into your spirit. Make no mistake; this kind of sweet seduction is deadly.

But I want to move in a different direction with this. Let's discuss another form of adultery. I want to address a kind of adultery that is asexual. This kind of affair is just as enticing, easier to accomplish, but still has the same defiling effects to our persons and even to God.

There are people within the Body of Christ who use their Bibles as the litmus test for all realities. Just a couple of days ago, we read how Jesus acknowledged the young scribes' and rabbis' skills with the Torah, but He also exposed their woeful lack of real relationship with the Father, God in the flesh, here and now.

These young men were taught early on that the Word of God is good. Rabbis would take a child's slate tablet and write these words: *"Oh taste and see that the Lord is good. How sweet are your words to my taste" (Psalm 34:8; Psalm 119:103, NASB)*. Then they would coat the tablet with honey and invite the child to lick up the sweet pleasure. It was an effective way of driving home the solid truth that God's Word is good stuff!

Did God never intended for the Bible be our primary lover?

Is it for our feeding, edification, and faith building? Yes, of course—all of these! But when we use the text to control and protect ourselves from anyone who might read the scriptures and interpret them differently, we open ourselves up to religious bondage that narrows our minds, our experiences, and most definitely, our influence.

Yes, read the Word of God! But if you approach every situation of your life with that big ole black book of yours, you might be the poster child at your church, but the rest of society probably wants nothing to do with you.

In the '90s, I was Senior Pastor of a church that was very prophecy focused and active for the Spirit. There were some crazy Sundays, and I honestly have to admit that up front.

There was a man who came every Sunday and always sat in the second row with his wife. She was all about everything going on in there. It didn't seem to be the same for him. He was always cordial, but I don't remember a single time in those eight years where he once made eye contact with me during ministry time. The man kept his eyes glued to his Bible.

You could just hear it in his head, *"There's no place like home. There's no place like home. There's no place like home."* Absolutely terrified. Some of the stuff manifesting in that room wasn't exactly in the ink.

It always saddened me because the river of the Spirit was often flowing through that room, and he never stepped out of his Bible-bubble long enough to experience what God was doing in that moment. That's a too common tale in the American Church.

In The Pages

What do you love more, your Bible or the Presence of God? Have you made any other substitutions for your personal relationship with your "first love"?

Lazy or Afraid?

November 6
Proverbs 6

"Go to the ant, O sluggard, observe her ways and be wise." Proverbs 6:6, NASB

There's a whole section in this chapter on laziness, slothfulness, indolence, idleness and being lackadaisical or lethargic. The Hebrew language refers to the *"sluggard"* in moral connotations. The idea is that being lazy is poor stewardship of the good gifts God has deposited in each of us.

Laziness is foolishness, as clearly stated in today's counsel. We get this. We all appreciate diligence, right?

We applaud hard work and accomplishment. We respect dedication and effort. We like winners, but we love a good underdog story too (I can hear the *"Rudy"* soundtrack playing in my head right now). I still cry like a sissy when they carry the leprechaun off the field. He didn't score the winning touchdown, nor did he intercept a game-saving pass!

But he got in the frikk'n game!

I recently read a blog post on laziness by Seth Godin[8], a secular marketing guru:

"I think laziness has changed. It used to be about avoiding physical labor. The lazy person could nap or have a cup of tea while others got hot and sweaty and exhausted. Part of the reason society frowns on the lazy is that this behavior means more work for the rest of us. When it came time to carry the canoe over the portage, I was always hard to find. The effort and the pain gave me two good reasons to be lazy. But the new laziness has nothing to do with physical labor and everything to do with fear. If you're not going to make those sales calls or invent that innovation or push that insight, you're not avoiding it because you need physical rest. You're hiding out because you're afraid of expending emotional labor. This is great news, because it's much easier to become brave about extending yourself than it is to become strong enough to haul an eighty pound canoe."

Godin might be on to something here.

How many of us calculate the costs before going the distance with our brothers and sisters? Are we really willing to go through their trials with them, climb those mountains, descend into those dark valleys? What are we so afraid of? Rejection? Pain? Emotional drainage? What? It can't be that we're just lazy, right? So what's the deal?

In The Pages

Rejection can also hype us for approval. Fear can cause us to fight, run away, or hide. What is going on with your energy meter today? Could it be real fatigue? Honestly, how is your health? Do you eat right, sleep enough, exercise, and live right with those around you? What needs to be corrected to get you back to balance?

Hey Joe!

November 7
Proverbs 7

"Her house is the way to hell, descending to the chambers of death." Proverbs 7:27, NKJV

HEY JOE
Billy Roberts © Third Palm Music (BMG), Used by Permission

Hey Joe, where you goin' with that gun in your hand?
Hey Joe, I said, where you goin' with that gun in your hand?
Alright. I'm goin' down to shoot my old lady,
You know I caught her messin' 'round with another man.
Hey Joe, I heard you shot your old lady down,
You shot her down to the ground.
Yes, I did, I shot her,
You know I caught her messin' 'round,
Messin' 'round town.

Frik! It's another proverb about the perils of adultery. Do you think Wisdom is trying to tell us something? I don't mind the repetitive discussions, because obviously this still isn't registering here!

How many marriages fail every day because infidelity has ripped those sacred covenants to shreds? If your life hasn't been affected in one way or another by divorce or the recklessness of illegitimate intimacy, consider yourself lucky. Most of us have experienced this stuff up close and personal.

History teaches us that we do play our dangerous games, but the problem is rarely another person.

The problem is mostly us.

Today's proverb personifies the whole concept of adultery. She puts her makeup on, lights a few candles, and waits on her bed in her dimly lit room.

Wisdom calls that place... that situation: *"hell."* Thus, the value of Wisdom's counsel is for us to realize that this story ends badly.

DEATH

Death to what?

It's the death of what is right, what is peaceful, what is alive in the light, and what is life-giving to those around us. When we engage in adulterous behavior, we take ourselves out of our God-sanctioned and God-protected environments and enter into these treacherous and unknown paths, only to discover darkness.

And for what... a few moments of sexual satisfaction? It is a path littered with destruction. It is a shortcut to the chambers of the grave.

"A young man involved in illicit sex may die from punishment meted out by an angry husband, or from poverty, or from venereal disease, or from spiritual and emotional anguish" (The Bible Knowledge Commentary, Proverbs 7:26-27).

Trust me, this is not a pretty picture.

Patti and I are close to too many men and women who still suffer the effects of these kinds of bad choices. It's heartbreaking. They live day in and day out with residuals from STD's, HIV, and other drastic life-altering complications, which are constant lingering reminders of those past choices.

They are ashamed. People do actually snap when illicit affairs are discovered. There are orphans in this world because an angry spouse killed their unfaithful partner before turning the gun on himself or herself. We know this truth up close and personal. Do you?

In The Pages

Is it worth it? What would you write in that commentary? Do you have a tale?

Prophesy Life

November 8
Proverbs 8

"Listen, for I will speak noble things; and the opening of my lips will produce right things." Proverbs 8:6, NASB

Most of what is going on in this chapter is Lady Wisdom making a case for us to receive and steward her qualities in our lives. Verse after verse, she encourages us to listen to her and to implement all aspects of what she unashamedly puts forth as wisdom.

Wisdom speaks *"noble things."* The word is **nâgîyd** (pronounced *naw-gheed'*), and it implies what Wisdom is saying comes from a position of authority. Think in terms of a military commander, an honorable governor, a chief ruler, a prince. Their words are a source of supremacy and influence. They push to the front of the line, not because they are arrogant or self-important, but because everyone gives way out of respect.

When Wisdom releases that authority, it produces *right things*, good things, things that are upright, just, and equitable.

So there He was, fresh out of the wilderness, having passed those early tests with Satan, sitting on the mountainside with throngs of people pressing into his every word, and the disciples inching ever closer for more revelation.

"He opened His mouth, and began to teach them." (Matthew 5:2, NASB)

From there, Jesus prophetically engaged them in a way unlike anything they had ever heard. It was Wisdom incarnate, bringing the message of the Kingdom. What I mean by "prophetically engaged" is that it was more than just an appeal to change their minds. This truth was so alive that it pressed into their spirit-man and messed them up.

He spoke with an authority that wrecked their hearts!

"When Jesus had finished these words, the crowds were amazed at His teaching; for He was teaching them as one having authority, and not as their scribes" (Matthew 7:28-29, NASB).

We've actually killed the meaning of the word *"amazed"* or "amazing" in our cheap and over-stimulated, yet starved word culture. The point is that the people were seized with panic. Everything they believed, everything they understood, their only paradigm they had about their "ok" with God had just been totally dismantled and disassembled before their very eyes and ears.

The Prince of Peace brought a prophetic disturbance that shook their old systems of false peace. It was a new beginning, a new way to experience truth. Authoritative wisdom can do that.

"Truly, truly, I say to you, he who believes in Me, the works that I do, he will do also; and greater works than these he will do; because I go to the Father," (John 14:12, NASB).

Out of Wisdom, we can stand in front of another person and prophesy words of life, hope, deliverance, and destiny. And then we get to see it take hold and bear fruit! Heck yeah!

In The Pages

Speaking life into someone else brings *you* life! When was the last time you spoke life over another person? How did that person react? What happened to you? Read 1 Corinthians 14:3. Come on! Find someone, call someone, or lay hands on someone. Release the words of life! Be a prince of deep wisdom that stirs and produces hope!

Solid Foundations

November 9
Proverbs 9

"Lady Wisdom has built and furnished her home; it's supported by seven hewn timbers." Proverbs 9:1, MSG

Proverbs 9 is a transitional chapter. It's basically a review or summary of the previous eight chapters. It's very simple and concise. The style changes in Proverbs 10 from thematic narrative to more of a random assortment of thoughts, each verse standing entirely on its own foundation of truth. Today's scripture is about two different women. One calls out for our good. The other calls out for our death. We decide which house we'll enter.

So again, Mama Wisdom invites us into her home. The chocolate chip cookies are cooling, the roast is in the oven, and homemade lemonade is ready to be poured. You can make the imagery whatever you want it to be. The point is that she has invited us all in with open, loving arms. It's about our growth and maturity, for those of us who still desire this kind of guidance.

I believe "table fellowship" is one of the best opportunities for real discipleship and spiritual basting. It creates opportunity for open and sincere sharing around a table, honest and vulnerable dialogue about the real stuff we face. Wisdom isn't laying down the rules for success. She genuinely cares that we grow up as blessed as possible.

The invitation is to partake and fill our plates with what we're willing to chew and digest. No one is forcing us to eat. There has to be some hunger on our part to taste what it is Wisdom is serving.

"It's supported by seven hewn timbers." The whole kitchen scene definitely warms the heart. But this is the part of the verse that appeals to our desire for internal strength.

I picture large cedar logs, much like the ones you would find in mountain cabins all over the Rockies. Seven is the number of completion, perfection, and finality in scripture. It is also the number of covenant, expressing itself through harmony, unity, blessing, and rest.

We see the seven churches in Revelation, representing the entire church. Isaiah 11:2 (NASB) mentions the seven gifts of the Spirit that reside upon the foretold Messiah:

> ***"the Spirit of the Lord,***
> ***the spirit of wisdom,***
> ***the spirit of understanding,***
> ***the spirit of counsel,***
> ***the spirit of strength,***
> ***the spirit of knowledge,***
> ***and the fear of the Lord"***

Don't let that cozy little kitchen fool you into thinking mama is just serving comfort food. Wisdom is supported by a great structure that actually has the Spirit of the Lord all over it. It's a solid foundation, strong and suitable enough to build a great life for yourself and your family. Which house are you going to enter?

In The Pages

When you think about asking for wisdom, what is your purpose? Is it for you and some decision you need to make, or is it wisdom for proper influence of others? Some would argue that real wisdom is Christ manifest in our processes. Do you agree with that? Why or why not?

Finish

November 10
Proverbs 10

"A wise youth harvests in the summer, but one who sleeps during harvest is a disgrace." Proverbs 10:5, NLT

Ok, so it was a really big deal back then for a son or daughter to act in a manner, which brought pride to a family, not shame. Harvest was one of those times when all hands were needed on deck. You pitched in whether you liked cucumbers or not, lettuce or not, beans or not, corn or not. You got the work done, and you probably did it with a smile on your face.

There are still some kids out there today who are under that same kind of family pressure to perform. Sports, academics, who you date, who you marry, cars, clothes—all the stupid stuff we put on our kids because we care about how it reflects on us.

A guy I run team with in ministry says, *"My generation has done just about everything we can do to screw up the next generation."* (That's not exactly how he says it... but even I have boundaries.) That feels very true sometimes. Sad... but VERY true.

It was different back then when Solomon's scribes penned those words. It was an agrarian culture; it was a matter of life and death to get the harvest in. It was unthinkable for any family member not to participate. Unthinkable!

Today's challenge is about finishing. Forget about the disgracing your family stuff. Focus on finishing what you start.

I had a coach in junior high school who, looking back now, was a disgrace to his profession.[9] He was a small man, skinny, loud mouth, sarcastic, and ruthless if you showed weakness of any sort. I doubt he ever played sports when he was in school.

As a kid, I suffered from fear. I wasn't much of a fan of physical contact, but football was practically a religion in small-town Texas. It was social suicide not to play. You'll be surprised to learn (I hope) that I was this skinny, weak, slow, extremely sheepish kid.

Coach never caught on to the fact that his yelling degrading insults at me didn't motivate me to try harder. Honestly, I just wanted to be on the team. I didn't care whether or not I played.

The guy was my coach for the next three years! Lovely.

My freshmen year of high school, our entire team was sitting in the locker room one day, waiting for our coaches to come in for the day's instructions. I happened to be talking to my buddy who was sitting next to me. When coach walked by, he turned his college ring around and slapped me on the back of my head. I saw frikk'n stars! I went home that day after practice, told my dad what happened, and begged him to let me quit for the fifteenth time. My dad decided to go up to the school to have a little chat with my nemesis, but the athletic director intervened before it escalated.

My dad had been a drill sergeant in the United States Army. He wasn't intimidated by my coach... not in the least. Anyway, my point is that my dad encouraged me to stay on the team, even when it got hard. You know what happened? I grew, I gained weight, and I eventually put on some muscle.

I ended up having a great high school experience with football. I'm glad I stuck with it. It really prepared me to be able to stare down some very hard things I would face in my future.

Hard, unfair, unjust, and plain ole rotten is not necessarily a good enough excuse to quit. Some of us need to toughen up, grow up, take responsibility, and finish what we've committed to. Even finish well!

In The Pages

Read Hebrews 12:2 (in the NASB or NKJV). What do you think "finisher" means? What is the hardest thing you have ever finished? Triumph or regret?

Needed Slap

November 11
Proverbs 11

"When pride comes, then comes dishonor, but with the humble is wisdom." Proverbs 11:2, NASB

"Therefore let him who thinks he stands take heed lest he fall. No temptation has overtaken you except such as is common to man; but God is faithful, who will not allow you to be tempted beyond what you are able, but with the

temptation will also make the way of escape, that you may be able to bear it."
1 Corinthians 10:12-13, NKJV

My first pastorate was at a little Baptist church in Central Texas. The first time they called me to preach, there was a record turnout of about 38 people in church that day. I had a couple hours commute back and forth between home and Seminary, but the church was only minutes from our parents and friends in Waco. It was a great place for Patti and I to grow up in the call.

My mentor and best friend at the time was the pastor of one of the largest Baptist churches in Waco.[10] He had seriously invested in me! He had as much to do with my spiritual development as anyone in my entire life.

Eventually, he encouraged me to "go for it," in terms of a life in full-time public ministry. It was only fitting the he and his church be the ones to ordain me into the gospel ministry.

We had a ritual. Friday was our day to hunt or fish together. I mean, every Friday! We spent hundreds, maybe thousands of hours together over the years.

One morning, with much pride and indignation in my voice, I asked him how another pastor of one of the largest Baptist churches in the SBC could possibly be so stupid and careless as to have an affair with a woman in his church, thus forfeiting his reputation and ministry for such ridiculous reasons.

Honestly, I was expecting him to say, *"Yeah, what a dumb ass!"* Instead, Mike gave me a stare that cut into my bones.

"Until you are exhausted, spent, worn down and very empty . . . until some hot young thing, who looks good and smells good, walks into your office and says to you, 'you turn me on' . . . until you have had to wrestle that devil, you would be wise to pray for him and not judge him."

I was absolutely (rightly so) nailed to the wall!
It wasn't mean. It was raw!

What my friend knew was that my own pride was setting me up for disaster. So he did what a mature and seasoned father lovingly does... he put the fear of God in me. It was a lesson that still replays over and over in my heart on a regular basis.

There is really no good excuse, only real sad reasons, why church leaders fall. We hear it all the time. My counsel echoes my friend's:

Let's exert wisdom and pray for our spiritual leaders (*and their spouses*)!

Do not judge them, stay humble, and avoid the pitfalls of pride.

In The Pages

How well do you think the Body of Christ handles such sad news of a moral failure with its membership and leaders? How do your own thoughts and actions need to change? Are you above temptation?

Puppy Love

November 12
Proverbs 12

"A righteous man regardeth the life of his beast: but the tender mercies of the wicked are cruel." Proverbs 12:10, KJV

"The angel of the Lord said to him, "Why have you struck your donkey these three times? Behold, I have come out as an adversary, because your way was contrary to me." Numbers 22:32, NASB

Patti and I have never really been pet people. Our daughters never asked for pets growing up, so we never really had a reason to get one. There were a few exceptions along the way, but for the most part, no pets.

But we do enjoy being in our friend's home. Their fourth son, Pudge (a jet black Shitzu/Poodle mix) is the perfect addition to their family (2010). As Michael says, *"That brother is high maintenance!"* I hear it takes one to know one.

Anyway, that little dog has quite the personality. Much like all the other boys in that house, he knows how to get Kathy to do exactly what he wants her to do. Whether he's begging for another potato chip, whining to go outside, or napping on the couch, Pudge attracts a lot of attention and receives lots of affection. He is fun to be around.

Once I got to futzing around with these passages, I was surprised to discover how much is written in scripture about man's responsibility to take care of our animals. The KJV says we are to *"regardeth"* them.

Normally, this is the kind of verse I would pass over very quickly with the notion that I fulfilled my responsibility to the pets I have had with food, water, and shelter. But the Hebrew word is **yâda'** (pronounced *yaw-dah'*) and it means, *"to know beyond what is casual."*

This kind of *"regard"* is sourced out of compassion—the kind of compassion a mother instinctively feels when she is growing a child in her womb! It conveys tender love, mercy, and even pity. Honestly, I was startled at how seriously God takes this issue.

We have a friend who is a major player in the Nashville music scene.[11] Years ago, Patti and I visited their home in rural Tennessee. I was surprised to discover they had a few farm animals. Don and his wife travel a lot with business and ministry. Christine explained her motivation for having those animals.

"It's good for me to have them. It requires me to naturally and emotionally give to them, knowing full-well they will not ever be able to say 'thank you' or show any sort of gratitude for what is required of me. It helps my character. I need them. They help ground me."

I had never heard anything like that. Considering how much time prophetic people spend up in the attic, it really is good to keep ourselves around natural need on a regular basis.

If God will go to the length of bringing a rebuke to Baalam through the mouth of a mule, it's probably a good thing for us to consider our ways and our hearts when it comes to the creatures that inhabit this earth with us. We can do better.

In The Pages

So what is your track record with your pets and animals? Have you ever been cruel to an animal? What are your thoughts about that now?

Insert Foot

November 13
Proverbs 13

"The one who guards his words guards his life, but whoever is talkative will come to ruin." Proverbs 13:3, NET

My grandparents had the most stellar garden out behind their house. The rich Arkansas Delta sandy loam was perfect for tomatoes, onions, black-eyed peas, okra, squash, corn, and many other kinds of vegetables. There were sliced beefsteak tomatoes on the table at every meal during the summers. What they didn't eat, Vera canned.

There were also fruit trees, strawberries, cantaloupes, and watermelons. That meant preserves, jellies, and cobblers!

I liked helping with all the harvesting, except with the blackberries. I seemed to spend more time fighting those thorns than I did picking berries. I swear that bush would actually reach out and grab you. It was kind of freaky.

Today's lesson is about paying attention to how we speak, how much we speak, and what we say. Scripture tells us to protect our words as we would protect our premises with a hedge of thorny blackberry bushes. The idea is that you can still get in and out, but you have to be careful. Pick the wrong place to enter, and you'll pay the consequences.

Many years ago, I was having lunch in a Mexican restaurant near Fort Worth with the guy that led worship at my church. Jeff is a skilled worship guy, but when he gets tickled, he gets the "anoinking," as he calls it. He snorts so loud; anyone within 75 feet of him can hear it. It's out of control.

There we were, chatting away, when I made eye contact with a woman I hadn't seen in 25 years. We were childhood friends. A six-foot tall wooden fence separated our backyards. But with a look... we recognized each other.

She walked straight to our table. I stood and hugged her and introduced her to Jeff. We chatted for a moment, and then I noticed she looked like she was about 5 months pregnant (it was a little pooch... that's all).

It never dawned on me that she might NOT be pregnant!

That was mistake #1. Then I asked (mistake #2), *"Wow, when is the baby due?"* while patting her belly (yes, I touched her)! Y'all, I meant that as a compliment! I love pregnant women and I think they are at the height of their beauty when they are with child.

Stone cold, she said, *"I'm not pregnant."* I felt all the blood drain from my face; I was nauseous and on the verge of puking in the chip basket! I have never wanted to crawl into a hole so badly in my entire life.

Jeff couldn't help himself and started snorting so loudly, they probably heard him in the kitchen. He buried his face in his napkin and just put his head down on the table.

"Kill me frikk'n now!"

Honestly, I don't think I said another word to her. I might have said something, but my ears were ringing so loudly, I have no memory of it. She just walked off... and I let her.

It was impossible to eat after that. Jeff couldn't stop snorting. I was afraid I was going to have to do the Heimlich on him or something. I tried to find her later to apologize, but she was gone. I'm sure she had lost her appetite too and succumbed to total shame and rejection.

Dear friend, if you are out there and you are reading this, I am SO sorry! Please forgive my stupidity!

Everyone else... please learn from my mistake. Slow down and guard your words.

In The Pages

Do people think you talk too much? How well do you listen? Do you ask for feedback about how much you run your mouth? Have you ever said something foolish you wish you could take back?

Manure

November 14
Proverbs 14

"Without oxen a stable stays clean, but you need a strong ox for a large harvest." Proverbs 14:4, NLT

"And now they're at it again! Take care of their threats and give your servants fearless confidence in preaching your Message, as you stretch out your hand to us in healings and miracles and wonders done in the name of your holy servant Jesus." Acts 4:29-30, MSG.

In Dr. Charles Ryrie's Study Bible, he says, *"There is no milk without some manure."* That's a much nicer way of putting it than what I would have used, but you get the point.

I was romantically naïve when I first got into ministry. I had a Bible verse for every problem, a nice little Christian antidote for every difficult situation. My insights were shallow and religious, and maybe they still are, but I've learned a few things since then.

Serving the Church can be challenging, to say the least. It took me a while to realize I was trying to fight every battle. I thought I had all the answers. Let me just say, some battles just aren't worth fighting.

The color of the carpet in the sanctuary, the administrative rule of the deacons, and how much to pay the janitor, just aren't good enough reasons to have to shovel crap out of the church. In a way, change and growth create problems. Reasonable stewardship has to cope with the increase. It's a good problem, I guess, but it stands to reason that as the congregation expands, we have to provide more care, more facilities, a bigger mortgage, and a bigger staff. It's just the way it is.

Where a lot of problems arise is in knowing that not everyone in the church is spiritual-minded. They see the church much as a country club... some "thing" to belong to.

They pay their dues, share their opinions, and pretty much feel entitled to run things as they see fit. Let's call that what it is:

MANURE

Now I remember why I was gray before I turned 40! Religious devils are still very much active in the church today! I'm willing to shovel the manure, but I want to know it is for the right reasons. Fighting with the "church" devils isn't too high on my agenda these days.

When the winds of the Spirit blow, waves of resistance will come. When the life of the Spirit explodes and life begins to manifest with power, there will always be a pushback from darkness. In fact, that's usually a good way to measure whether or not you are going in the right direction.

If you want it neat, if you can't handle the mess, stay with religion.

If you want the real, if you want to see Him move with power, if you really do want God to do things His way and you desire to give the Spirit permission to move, then watch out! It's going to get a little crazy up in here!

Why? Because the real stuff always exposes the fake. Life is contrast to death. Health brings light to sickness. The fullness of His presence fills the void. Blow, wind, blow! Come, Spirit, come!

But yeah, have your shovel ready.

In The Pages

See *1 Peter 4:12-14*. How does this relate to today's topic? Seriously, what do you want: nice, comfortable religion, or to get down to the real business? Are you willing to pay whatever it costs?

Stupid Is — Stupid Does

November 15
Proverbs 15

"He who profits illicitly troubles his own house, but he who hates bribes will live." Proverbs 15:27, NASB

Then Joshua and all Israel with him, took Achan the son of Zerah, the silver, the mantle, the bar of gold, his sons, his daughters, his oxen, his donkeys, his sheep, his tent and all that belonged to him; and they brought them up to the valley of Achor. Joshua said, "Why have you troubled us? The Lord will trouble you this day." And all Israel stoned them with stones; and they burned them with fire after they had stoned them with stones. They raised over him a great heap of stones that stands to this day, and the Lord turned from the fierceness of His anger. Therefore the name of that place has been called the valley of Achor to this day" Joshua 7:24-27, NASB

It's a brutal story. Under the old covenant, there were very strict rules about these kinds of things. Jericho was the first of ten cities to be conquered after Israel crossed over into its promise.

God gave the Israelites a plan for capturing the city. Not one man was lost. It was supernatural and evident that God was with them. But there were instructions on what to do with the spoils left in the city.

None of the goodies were to be taken. Everything was to be dedicated to the Lord. Everyone understood the seriousness of it... except Achan.

*"So Achan answered Joshua and said, "Truly, I have sinned against the Lord, the God of Israel, and this is what I did: when I saw among the spoil a beautiful mantle from Shinar and two hundred shekels of silver and a bar of gold fifty shekels in weight, then I **coveted them** and **took them**; and behold, they are concealed in the earth inside my tent with the silver underneath it"* (Joshua 7:20-21, NASB).

Whew... that's ugly right there! He *"coveted"* and *"took,"* which released a firestorm of hell on the whole camp, resulting in the death of his entire family!

It's interesting. Jericho, a fortified city, fell with a trumpet blast. The next city to be taken was Ai. It was nothing more than a tiny village. It was supposed to be a simple raid, easy enough for a few skilled soldiers to handle. It ended up being a total disaster because of one guy's greed!

The single bar of gold Achan took out of Jericho is the equivalent to stealing one Timex out of Tiffany & Co. warehouse. Compared to the bulk, it's not much. But sized up against HIS instructions, it became a very large problem for everyone!

The bottom-line here is this:

The entire operation was a "faith" thing.

Israel had moved out in faith, trusting that God was with them, and evidently He was. But there was an integrity crisis that compromised the partnership. God did His part. Israel? Well, it wasn't good.

How many times have you and I moved towards something we felt God was leading us to, yet we were unwilling to act totally in faith?

So you want to make a living with your computer and you are asking God for His blessing on your business? Awesome! How much of your software is pirated? Are your customers really yours, or did you bring them over from your last job? Are your expense receipts really accurate? What about your tax returns? Have we profited "illicitly," or do we know that God's hand has provided and blessed our faithful integrity?

Those who desire the deepest touches of intimacy and favor from the Lord care about all of those kinds of things.

In The Pages

My personal experience has taught me that calculated "shortcuts" to save money, time, or trouble, release much stress in my heart. How about you? What lessons have you learned that you would want your family to benefit from through your understanding and failures on this topic? See Genesis 14:22-24. What is this about?

Heart Scrubbing

November 16
Proverbs 16

"Everyone who is proud in heart is an abomination to the Lord; assuredly, he will not be unpunished." Proverbs 16:5, NASB

"Man, proud man, drest in a little brief authority, most ignorant of what he's most assur'd, glassy essence, like an angry ape, plays such fantastic tricks before high heaven, as make the angels weep." William Shakespeare

This *"proud in heart"* thing is a serious issue. One of the biggest problems is that we rarely see it in ourselves. God has to reveal it to us in an up-close-and-personal kind of way. It's a bad day when He decides to deal with our pride. You won't like it. Trust me. You will NOT like it!

Remember when your mom would grab the washcloth and go to work on the grime behind your ears? It's the same thing, only the scrubbing is on your heart. Shakespeare had it right. The angels weep, because they know the process we're going to have to go through to have our eyes opened to our own demise.

Tôw'êbâh (pronounced *to-ay-baw'*) is the Hebrew word for *"abomination."* The overall implication is that something is disgusting to the Lord. This is the same word used to describe the Lord's abhorrence to idols.

What's so offensive to Him is that we have made our idol out of our own wants and desires. It's our own little private god—an attitude, our religion, some skewed spiritual expression made specifically to suit us. You're not going to enjoy where this is going. I don't either, because it's repulsive.

The source of such arrogance and insolence is very clear:

"How you are fallen from heaven, O shining star, son of the morning! You have been thrown down to the earth, you who destroyed the nations of the

world. For you said to yourself, 'I will ascend to heaven and set my throne above God's stars. I will preside on the mountain of the gods far away in the north. I will climb to the highest heavens and be like the Most High'" (Isaiah 14:12-14, NLT).

This was exactly Lucifer's issue: PRIDE

He was unwilling to honor and give thanks to his Creator. The Apostle Paul wrote to the church in Rome, expressing his disgust of such behavior. Here are a few of his thoughts:

"*Yes, they knew God, but they wouldn't worship him as God or even give him thanks. And they began to think up foolish ideas of what God was like. As a result, their minds became dark and confused. Claiming to be wise, they instead became utter fools. And instead of worshiping the glorious, ever-living God, they worshiped idols made to look like mere people and birds and animals and reptiles*" (Romans 1:21-23, NLT).

If you read that entire chapter (Romans 1) for contextual purposes, you'll find that the Apostle Paul was pretty wound up. I sit in judgment of no one, but there is some pretty terse language that could be applicable to our world even today.

I'm not saying I have the answers. I'm just suggesting we should probably be asking more questions. Honestly, I sometimes struggle with how contrary culture lives to the warnings in scripture. It can be a bit confusing out there.

Overall, to have pride in our hearts is not a good thing. He will eventually deal ruthlessly with such vanity. There is no escaping the divine scrubbing that is surely to come.

In The Pages

Has anyone ever told you that you have pride? What was your reaction? What course of action have you taken to deal with the accusation? Was it legit?

Disco Inferno

November 17
Proverbs 17

"The refining pot is for silver and the furnace for gold, but the Lord tests the hearts." Proverbs 17:3, NKJV

"Do you see what I've done? I've refined you, but not without fire. I've tested you like silver in the furnace of affliction. Out of myself, simply because of who I am, I do what I do. I have my reputation to keep up. I'm not playing second fiddle to either gods or people." Isaiah 48:10-11, MSG

Back in the '80s, we were first starting to put down our hymnals and sing with uplifted hands and hearts to the lyrics splattered across big screens in the sanctuary. This was quite the scandal back then in many churches. One song we sang was called *Refiner's Fire*. Sometimes I wonder just how much refining fire I've prophetically invited into my life from singing that one song as often as we did! Eish!

Here is yet another reminder that the Lord is eager to cut the crap out of our heart. The Hebrew word for *"tests"* is directly tied to the furnace and the refining pot. We are talking serious heat here!

Picture God turning up the heat to remove chaff and strain out impurities, thus increasing the value of what He is working on inside of us. The **mitsrêph** (pronounced *mits-rafe'*), or *"refining pot,"* was the actual container the smith put the metal in.

With the precious metal confined inside that crucible, the refining pot was then placed in the **kûwr** (pronounced *koor*), or *"furnace,"* nestled in the coals at the bottom of the kiln. It was superheated with fire to melt the ores until all impurities floated to the surface.

If God really *is* after the refinement of our heart, our character, and how we love and relate to others, HE can bring that same heat in many different ways. Internal pressures, external agitations, delays, relational complexities, expenses in real covenant, sickness, weakness, wilderness wanderings, and plain old hardship, pain, and suffering.

All this because you want to be used by Him!

Fire isn't always about punishment. More times than not, it comes because you got a word or a promise from God, and you want to go for it! It may not feel like it when you are in the process of being refined, but He does this because He is madly in love and crazy about you!

A lot of my life's message is about fire, furnaces, pressures, purging dross, floating flotsam (look it up), and the disposing of pride. We all want a word, we all want a promise, and we all want the prize or the fruit of God's faithful promise. But God uses that time in between the promise and the reward to go to work on us.

That time slot is called "fire."

If you can embrace and endure your time of being in that furnace, without defiling yourself or blaspheming God, you'll be a new product, polished inside and out.

In The Pages

How do you respond when the heat gets turned up? Honestly, are you a complainer? Do you shut down? Do you medicate? Or do you keep moving with a good attitude? What is your fire about right now? How you doing in that kiln?

When the heat is on us, it's easy to think that God must be displeased with us somehow. God isn't burning the dross in order to make us more loveable. God could be burning the things in us that create hardships for ourselves. A form of medicine for our restoration and healing. —MDP 2018

Shut Yo Pie Hole

November 18
Proverbs 18

"A fool does not delight in understanding, but only in revealing his own mind." Proverbs 18:2, NASB

"Fools care nothing for thoughtful discourse; all they do is run off at the mouth." Proverbs 18:2, MSG

This may be a little prickly for some of you, but hang with me today. I know who my audience is. If you'll open up your hearts and allow today's message to mess with you, it will create a channel that will allow you access to the people and passions you want to learn from. Believe me... that will benefit you greatly.

In the spiritual culture Patti and I live in, having a mentor or coach is a big interest among today's young adults. We rarely call it discipleship anymore, but that's what it is. In this crazy world we live in, where time is the currency of our existence, it is extremely costly (both emotionally and spiritually) to be a spiritual mentor to a young adult who is not your own kid. We do it because we love it.

We love the people who pull on us. It is one of the most natural and rewarding things we have ever done. But developing those relationships, exercising that trust, sharing intimate details of our mistakes, opening up, exposing our spirits, is real work and very tiring.

Let me say again, it is what we (Patti and myself) do, what we love, and we know God is all over it. I am not complaining, only shedding light on what it costs to live like that.

Today's focus verse got me going on this. A fool doesn't recognize the seriousness of a situation or grasp the importance of an opportunity when it is right in front of them.

I don't like the word *"fool"* because it just seems overly rude, even for me. But it is what it is.

When you meet up with your mentor for coffee, do you come to the table with questions and probing thoughts, ready to heed counsel? Or do you come eager to share all of your own ideas and demonstrate your vast knowledge?

IF you are truly looking to be discipled, it is absolutely vital for you to consider your approach. A real mentor is someone who truly desires to give you "the goods," but more importantly, his or her time.

Richard Rohr[12], a globally recognized Christian teacher and author, often teaches that our aged culture has been too eager to sow into the ego of the young learner. We promote the expulsion of the under-experienced ideas much too quickly.

Most eastern cultures require their avid learners, those who hope to gain wisdom and maturity, to be quiet in the discipleship process. Thoughtful questioning is much more respected than the projection of personal ideas. In that culture, students never relate information to their mentors as they would to a peer. Being around elders is a time to inquire, listen, and ponder new realities. It's a perfect opportunity to honor the voice of experienced wisdom and time-tested truth.

Don't worry; there are ***millions*** of ways for your voice to be heard these days. But to gain truth experientially through a loving mentor relationship is rare and precious!

Wisdom advises: **HANDLE WITH CARE!**

Say "thank you" often. Really mean it.

In The Pages

Assess your desires. Do you just need a friend or someone to listen to you? Do you need a part-time counselor? Or do you desire the growth and stretching of real discipleship? Go back and read today's verses again. What else do you see?

Touching Skeletons

November 19
Proverbs 19

"The one who is gracious to the poor lends to the Lord, and the Lord will repay him for his good deed." Proverbs 19:17; NET

The Hebrew word for *"gracious"* is **chânan** (pronounced *khaw-nan´*) meaning, *"one who lowers his or her self in humility to the level of the one in need."* It's the raw mercy, sympathy, and compassion for the pain and desperation of another.

It's taking pity on someone, knowing that what you give will never be repaid. There is no hope of reward, recognition, or reimbursement—only an outpouring of grace.

In today's focus verse, the *"poor"* are the physically hungry. The word *dal* literally means, *"dangling."* Barely hanging on because of being *"weak, lean, skinny, emaciated, and waiflike."*

We don't see too much of this here in the United States.

People may not always have the resources to eat the most nutritious foods, but we can usually get food somewhere: homeless shelters, food banks, soup kitchens, etc. Today's proverb is talking about another level of need altogether. Walking skeletons wasting away, in dire need of the most basic elements for survival.

Jesus had a lot to say on this topic. It's not something we can ignore. Kingdom is not just about the spectacular future—*"Come Lord Jesus, come!"* We are responsible for reality around us today. Denial is not an option we can afford.

*"Then the King will say to those on His right, 'Come, you who are blessed of My Father, inherit the kingdom prepared for you from the foundation of the world. For I was hungry, and you gave Me something to eat; I was thirsty, and you gave Me something to drink; I was a stranger, and you invited Me in; naked, and you clothed Me; I was sick, and you visited Me; I was in prison, and you came to Me.' Then the righteous will answer Him, 'Lord, when did we see You hungry, and feed You, or thirsty, and give You something to drink? And when did we see You a stranger, and invite You in, or naked, and clothe You? When did we see You sick, or in prison, and come to You?' The King will answer and say to them, 'Truly I say to you, **to the extent that you did it to one of these brothers of Mine, even the least of them, you did it to Me'"*** (Matthew 25:34-40, NASB).

It's obvious Jesus is asking his disciples to care about the most basic needs (natural and spiritual) of mankind. We get stuck in our shtick. It's most helpful when we're sensitive enough to evaluate the real hunger around us. A famished man might be more prone to consider our gospel tract AFTER we've handed him some bread.

The woman with the sign at the intersection, asking for food money, isn't interested in your religious propaganda. These walking skeletons (natural and spiritual) are everywhere.

What do we DO about them?

Can we overcome our addiction to comfort and really focus on them? Jesus agrees with what Wisdom is saying today. God pays attention to our responses to the *poor*, the hungry, the naked, the estranged, and, yes, even the prisoner.

HE sees all of that. Ministry to them is ministry to HIM. Our meeting real needs for people with grace, dignity, and simple love are the basic elements of Kingdom consciousness.

In The Pages

Are you touching any skeletons? Where can you start? When can you start? Will you start?

Cutting Deep

November 20
Proverbs 20

"Whoever curses his father or his mother, his lamp will be put out in deep darkness." Proverbs 20:20, NKJV

We tend to think of this in terms of the words we speak. That's definitely one kind of *curse*, but we're going to need to expand our understanding here in order to get the full weight of today's warning.

The word for *"curses"* in today's text is **qâlal** (pronounced ***kaw-lal'***) and it means, *"to be light."* Not like sunlight, but light as in, *"to take lightly, to treat worthlessly, or to act towards another contemptuously."*

At the time Solomon wrote this, the Law was pretty unforgiving on this issue (Exodus 21:17; Leviticus 20:9; Deuteronomy 27:16). The punishment was death! I guess that pretty much took care of being a smart-ass to your parents.

So let's take a look at this whole *"lamp"* imagery with the ancient Hebrew. According to theologians, this is called a hypocatastasis, which is a fancy way of saying, *"an implied comparison."* The *lamp* was your life. When the light went out, it was the end of your life (physical, emotional, spiritual, and all the influence thereof). A deep *darkness* was all you were left with.

The word for *"darkness"* is **chôshek** (pronounced *koh-shek'*), and it implies *"misery, destruction, obscurity, and finality." "Deep darkness"* was the epicenter of darkness, the-center-of-your-pupil dark—an absolute and total dark. You feeling me here? You need to. Not out of fear, but out of a desire to be light and love to others, just as He has been light and love to us.

Solomon isn't talking about hell. He's referring to a life forfeit of love and light. Being at odds with or in total opposition to the people who birthed you is a form of hell on earth. Separation from one or more parents may or may not be within your control, but *"cursing"* them most certainly is.

I've heard too many ugly stories about what some kids have had to go through. Abuse, incest, abandonment—it's all too common. Patti and I have experienced first-hand the process of helping some of these kids learn to cope, heal, and reconcile.

Unlike other kids, these kids didn't have the luxury of being able to turn to their parents in the midst of tragedy for comfort. So we give them grace as they process, when they act out, and even when they manifest their own dysfunctions. When kids like this do not have a kingdom influence to help them process some of this stuff, they will likely continue down their own destructive paths.

Even if you feel like you got handed the rawest of deals, if you have some measure of Kingdom influence, and you've caught the wind of the Spirit, you still have to choose whether or not you want to live in a positive reality.

Those of us who get that know that we too, have been forgiven much, probably when we didn't deserve it. Therefore, we have a responsibility to forgive others and extend some grace.

I'm not implying that anyone continue to submit himself or herself to abuse. I'm saying we must find that inner strength and heart of Christ to convey honor and blessing wherever we can. We cannot allow the spirit of rejection (anger, control, and bitterness) to rule over us any longer. We have to face the realities of our circumstances (good, bad, or ugly) and still choose to be an outflow of living water.

Believe me, our parents don't really believe they did a perfect job raising us. For most of you, they never intended to harm you or cause you pain.

Can you see past your own hurt and ask God to show you theirs?

Do you know your parents' childhood stories? Can you start to see that some of this goes back a long way and doesn't really have anything to do with you? Can you see that what caused your greatest pain could possibly be redeemed and used for some ultimate good?

Can you see? Will you even try to see?

In The Pages

Honestly, how are you doing with all of this? What is your plan to change your course? How much healing do you have with this? Read Matthew 15:4-6. What point do you think Jesus is trying to make?

Always Pissed

November 21
Proverbs 21

"Better to dwell in a corner of a housetop, than in a house shared with a contentious woman." Proverbs 21:9, NKJV

"It is better to live in a desert land than with a contentious and vexing woman." Proverbs 21:19, NASB

Before I get into this, I want to take a moment to say thank you to my wife. This is not, and for the most part never has been, a problem in our house. I have been blessed beyond words with a wife who cares about having the presence of God in our home. She takes it upon herself to steward her part in facilitating our passions to the best of her abilities. She sets the tone beautifully, and has been a fabulous role model to our daughters who desire this same peace in their homes! Thanks babe!

Just about anything is better than living with a *"contentious woman"* (*Proverbs 19:13; 25:24; 27:15*). A *contentious woman* is an angry woman, the exact opposite of a woman who is content and at peace.

The KJV paints her as a *brawler*. The Hebrew describes this woman as *"agitated, prone to quarreling, nagging, quick to engage in strife."* Contemporary language would just call her *bitchy*.

Wisdom tells us to avoid sharing living space with this woman at all costs. It would be safer to approach the wild beast outside, than to approach the beast inside.

Back then, most Middle Eastern homes had a small room up on the roof that could be used for a variety of purposes. Hiding from the grating havoc inside was a sad and often lonely, but viable, option.

Honestly, this hurts my heart some. Maybe I'm just a chauvinist and naïve in my vain assumptions, but I don't think this is what God pictured when He created Eve. If a woman is manifesting these kinds of traits, something is wrong. She's probably endured some things that have influenced her sour attitude and behavior.

Is this really her idea of womanhood? To make everyone around her so miserable that they either succumb to her demands and abuse, or stay out of her way altogether? Why has this woman lost her softness? Why the edge?

Dear sister, daughter, or wife,

Your strength is welcomed in our life. Your courage is acknowledged. But your way does not promote the life and blessing God created you to display.

You are to be the glory of your mate.

You are to be the representation and shadow of the Bride of Christ!

You are the magnificent and glorious creation of God's intentioned will and purpose!

Are you willing to muster the courage to see how everyone acts and feels around you?

Do your children feel loved by you, or do they experience your wrath more often than not?

Does your family tread lightly when you are nearby, or do you put them at ease with the warmth and love from your bosom?

In The Pages

There is something in this for every one of us. Guys, does the woman in your life manifest *"contentions"* because of your selfish weaknesses? Madame, why the anger? Please seek out a friend, tell your story, and purge your poisons! We need the Lord's tender touch through you!

Blind and Chained

November 22
Proverbs 22

"Thorns and snares are in the way of the perverse; he who guards himself will be far from them." Proverbs 22:5, NASB

I have mulled over this verse a little longer than usual today. I feel the Lord pressing on me to bring some weight to today's devotional. There is a lot going on here.

"Thorns and snares" speak directly to what impedes and hinders progress. *Thorns* entangle and obstruct; *snares* trap and encase. These are the obstacles that stand in the way of the *perverse*.

This particular imagery of the *snare* is that of a spring trap, a net hidden under leaves. As unsuspecting animals venture into the net to sample the bait, they trip the snare and are caught, helplessly suspended from any means of escape. The word for *perverse* is ʿ**iqqêsh** (pronounced *ik-kashe´*) meaning, *"distorted, twisted, contrary, and the hidden false."* Let me see if I can increase the heat on this flame a bit.

The image above is a painting by German artist, Lovis Corinth.[13] It's entitled, **Samson**. This image has messed with me for some time now.

Several years ago, I was looking for some clipart for a sermon illustration, and I ran across this painting. It so interested me that I bought a book on the artist, read it, and tried to understand his story. I am still very moved by this painting.

The mighty man (who had once been dedicated to God by his parents) is reduced to blindness and bondage due to his *perverse* and stupid choices. Personally, I think this is an accurate picture for way too many young men and women who fail to realize just how much bondage results from their poor choices.

The church legalistically tells us all the things that are absolutely wrong, when really some of it might be ok. But the world and Hollywood tells us that **everything** is all right when we know some of those things are not beneficial for anyone! We know it! Not just because of what the Bible or some hotheaded preacher says about it, but because we know it in our heart! It's askew, twisted, and yup... downright *perverse*.

So are we just going to ignore this? Is that our approach when the questions get uncomfortable for us? Compared to our Holy Jesus, the entire world is a piece of gutter poo. Even so, Father God loves the gutter poo of this world. It's hard to imagine, but HE does.

Jesus (His Son) never ever really got caught up in pointing out people's sin. Even His frontal assaults on the religious aristocracy were more about their blind hypocrisy than their moral *perversion*.

HIS way, which was different from the normal religious patterns (abused and diverted as they were), was to encourage people to receive something different. He was very well aware of their sin, but would offer them something else instead, something less cumbersome.

He brought light into their darkness. Boys and girls, the best we've got is to let the love and light of Jesus shine through our lives! You don't have the time and energy to point out everyone's sin. They already know about their issues. People aren't stupid.

Show them Jesus. Give them the Light. Give His love to everyone until they're ready to change their mind!

In The Pages

Seriously, look at that painting again. Now imagine it's your face behind that stained blindfold. What is it that puts you in such a position? Is your strength being stolen? What is your plan to escape from *perverse* pain?

I don't judge Sampson here. It's too painful to judge. "If not for the grace of God..." Paul reminds us that, "All things are permissible..." In other words, God can handle our "falling short" and still love and accept us deeply, but we have to own the truth about our lives. The second part of Paul's quote is: "But not all things are profitable." God didn't put the chains on Samson.

Samson put the chains on himself. That's messed up and unfortunate. Samson is the reason he's blind and chained. Not God. —MDP 2018

Saying #18

November 23
Proverbs 23

"Who are the people who are always crying the blues? Who do you know who reeks of self-pity? Who keeps getting beat up for no reason at all? Whose eyes are bleary and bloodshot? It's those who spend the night with a bottle, for whom drinking is serious business. Don't judge wine by its label, or its bouquet, or its full-bodied flavor. Judge it rather by the hangover it leaves you with—the splitting headache, the queasy stomach. Do you really prefer seeing double, with your speech all slurred, reeling and seasick, drunk as a sailor? 'They hit me,' you'll say, 'but it didn't hurt; they beat on me, but I didn't feel a thing. When I'm sober enough to manage it, bring me another drink!'" Proverbs 23:29-35, MSG

If there wasn't so much truth to this passage, it could almost be considered comical. Whether it's Otis spending the night in the Mayberry jail, or Brooks Foster slurring through his pretend drunken monologue, we rarely feel the raw effects of a drunk. That is, unless you have resided with one, were raised by one, or you're currently married to one.

Between Proverbs 22:17 and Proverbs 24:34, there are 36 "sayings" of wisdom I would encourage any person, young or old, to memorize, store in their heart, and keep ready on their lips at all times. Today's verses (the 18th saying) are included in that collection.

It's formulated as a riddle. There are six questions that reveal six effects of repetitive alcohol abuse. Four are emotional: ***woe, sorrow, contentions, and complaints***. The other two are physical: ***bruised*** and ***bloodshot eyes***.
Wisdom also discusses the impairment of judgment: ***seeing things, hearing things,*** and ***putting oneself in situations that could be potentially hazardous***. The subject is left feeling hung-over, seeing his or her own demise . . . only to recycle the addiction again tomorrow.

This is not an anti-drinking plea. I enjoy an adult beverage as much as the next person. Yes, I know that "some" of the church has issues with it, but there is no such agreement from the bulk of the Body.

Most fundamental evangelicals have done just about everything they can do to minimize and discredit the facts around Jesus' first public miracle. It was a party, a sacred celebration of covenant for heaven's sake. Can we please cut the crap? It wasn't just medicinal, nor was it always watered down. It was wine, not Welch's. Help us, Lord!

If you elect not to drink alcohol, that's your choice, and I totally respect it. But don't manipulate the scripture to say something it doesn't say.

What we're talking about today is a whole other level of drinking. We are talking about an addiction. We are talking about the loss of stewardship and responsibility, which has this person out of touch with all reality.

There is help out there—ministries and professional services that offer all kinds of help. But that person (your friend, your family member, your spouse, maybe even you) has to be committed to getting sober. Quick fixes rarely, if ever work.

In The Pages

If you grew up around alcohol abuse, it probably left a lasting impression on you. How? What alterations have you made to your life as a result of those memories? Has it helped you? Do you know a person and/or family that needs your prayers now on this issue?

Big Bad Wolves

November 24
Proverbs 24

"Rescue the perishing; don't hesitate to step in and help. If you say, "Hey, that's none of my business," will that get you off the hook? Someone is watching you closely, you know—Someone not impressed with weak excuses."
Proverbs 24:11-12, MSG

RESCUE THE PERISHING
(Francis J. Crosby, 1869)

Rescue the perishing, care for the dying,
Snatch them in pity from sin and the grave;

Weep o'er the erring one, lift up the fallen,
Tell them of Jesus, the mighty to save.
Rescue the perishing, care for the dying,
Jesus is merciful, Jesus will save!

In Peterson's "Conversations" edition of The Message, he asks a viable question: *"Is wisdom just for me?"* He goes on, *"...we have to break down the wall of self-preservation that separates us from the needs of those around us."* Amen Brother Eugene... AMEN!

The church is absolutely locked-up with fear of the big bad wolf.

Huff and puff all you want, but we are all safe and secure inside our big ole stained glass fortress. Meanwhile, what about the rest of the outside world? Wolves are devouring them! Are we going to do something?

Most of us are willing to write a check to our local missionary friend or neighbor, but *"please Lord, don't send me out there! I can't afford to be soiled by all that filth, disease and pain."* Hmmmmmmm.

Several English translations encourage us to help the **môwṭ** (pronounced *mote*), those who are *"slipping,"* staggering and tottering on thin lines of sin, disease, war, famine or mortal danger. We are called to get involved in social justice issues, both here at home and abroad. Peterson points us to how Jesus did it:

"Put yourself aside, and help others get ahead. Don't be obsessed with getting your own advantage. Forget yourselves long enough to lend a helping hand. Think of yourselves the way Christ Jesus thought of himself. He had equal status with God but didn't think so much of himself that he had to cling to the advantages of that status no matter what. Not at all. When the time came, he set aside the privileges of deity and took on the status of a slave, became human! Having become human, he stayed human. It was an incredibly humbling process. He didn't claim special privileges. Instead, he lived a selfless, obedient life and then died a selfless, obedient death—and the worst kind of death at that—a crucifixion." (Philippians 2:3-8, MSG)

It might help to read that again... slowly.

I can't help but think that these verses in Philippians should be the foundational bedrocks of covenantal community. What great themes! *"Regard one another as more important than yourselves (Philippians 2:3, NASB).* What if we actually did this?

What would happen if we treated those "out there" as if they were more important than ourselves?

The word for *"regard"* is **hēgĕŏmai** (pronounced *hayg-eh´-om-ahee*), which implies to treat others with such respect, it's as if we are in the presence of a chief ruler or royalty. That was Jesus' way. He *"emptied Himself"* (Philippians 2:7, NASB).

Kĕnŏō (pronounced *ken-ŏ´-o*) suggests the absolute neutralization of all ego influence. Perfection, God with skin, set it all aside so He could approach us in a way that would put us at ease. That's how real internal transactions take place. He was a master of this process.

We know we are called to make a difference, to care about what no one else seems to care about and to go where no one else seemingly wants to go. But *how* we go matters.

If I'm full of myself, I'm dead in the water before I even get there. But if I empty myself and do it in *His* Love, in *His* way, I've got a chance at bringing some light to some very dark places.

In The Pages

What do you see that's unjust? What pulls at your heart? What is your plan to get involved?

Intentioned Humility

November 25
Proverbs 25

"Don't work yourself into the spotlight; don't push your way into the place of prominence. It's better to be promoted to a place of honor than face humiliation by being demoted." Proverbs 25:6-7, MSG

In Proverbs 25, Solomon separates his advice into four areas of focus: **humility in front of kings, prudence around neighbors, grace towards enemies,** and **self-discipline**. That first topic, *humility around kings*, is interesting. Since we don't have a king, it's easy for us to blow this off, but we really do need to pay attention to this.

This is the second time I've referenced this passage. No apologies here. Make it a double! We really need to get this.

In the summer of 1999, a few minister friends and I had the opportunity to attend a private speech by the Governor of Texas, George W. Bush. He was only a couple of weeks away from announcing his candidacy for President.

We eagerly awaited his arrival as the security detail took their positions throughout the room. When the Governor finally arrived, the actual weight of his presence was overwhelming! The entire room came to life!

I remember thinking beforehand, *"I must be a pretty big deal to get invited to such a strategic gathering."* But when he walked in, I instantly felt very small and insignificant in that setting.

We sat in a circle. He answered questions and expounded on some of his ideas, and then he asked us to pray for him. We gathered around him, laid hands, prophesied, prayed, and cried for him. I actually felt I had a word from the Lord for the man.

As we were shaking hands goodbye, I shared that word with him. He bore his eyes into mine and then thanked me and hugged me in a very genuine way. I knew I had touched on something authentic.

That was my one and only encounter with what I think Solomon was talking about. I have often wondered about the "electricity" in the room that day. Forget politics, because I'm not even remotely interested in the discussion here.

Whatever you have to say about our former president (and I know not everyone agrees) God's hand was on that man (Romans 13:1)! Right or wrong, good or bad, loved or hated, President Bush was the steward of the highest office in the United States of America for eight years. Whether we agree with his politics or not, it is important for us to remain humble around the responsibility of the office! The same applies for our current President.

In Luke 14:7-11, Jesus saw something that disturbed Him enough to address the group as a whole. His instruction was very cutting and precise:

Cultivate an attitude of honor,

Stop promoting yourself,

Prefer others before yourself,

And don't be quick to assume your place is at the head of the table.

Wisdom encourages us to figure this out for ourselves, rather than have to face the humiliating consequences of being "put in our places." Wearing a "disgraced face" is painful!

In the Pages

How intentional are you in giving honor where you can, as you should? Honor is not worship. What is the difference? Today's passage reminds us that honor given eventually results in honor received. Record you thoughts on this concept.

Shooting the Bird

November 26
Proverbs 26

"Like a sparrow in its flitting, like a swallow in its flying, so a curse without cause does not alight." Proverbs 26:2, NASB

I have to give credit where credit is due. My good friend Michael preaches a great message entitled, *"Offenses."*[14] That sermon has really made some connections for me when it comes to this proverb.

I've known these principles a long time, but his skill in being able to apply the text to real life is what really helped me gain a deeper understanding of what Wisdom wants us to take away from this. My friends teach me constantly.

The message begins with the problem of *taking in* an offense when we're wronged. When we harbor an offense without really offering forgiveness and grace from our heart, it becomes a **wound**.

That wound leads to **bitterness**, which leads to **defilement**, which leads to **despising**, which leads to **disloyalty**, which eventually leads to **hate**, which Jesus says is equivalent to **murder** (Matt 5:21-22).

But it doesn't have to play out like this!

We can forgive and release whomever and whatever it was that hurt us. That brings us healing and, ultimately, freedom. This is basic kingdom protocol. We must choose to forgive. It's not nuclear physics.

The problem is rarely whatever it was that just offended us (*the curse*). We make it about that, but it goes much deeper. The bigger issue is that we are carrying around these unhealed wounds we haven't dealt with yet (*the cause*). And when someone offends us (*the curse*), it exposes some of these unhealed wounds (*the cause*) and ignites a chain reaction.

With so many of these wounds at the surface, we become easily offended and quickly set off. It's a breeding ground, an easy target for the enemy. Unhealed, we get so dog piled and heavy-burdened; it's impossible to achieve peace with anything or anyone. We become the perch for the *"flitting sparrow"* to land on.

We poison ourselves. A sparrow is a very small, light, weightless creature. Often, our defilement happens without us realizing what we've done to ourselves.

What should be brushed off as if it were a gnat ends up hitting us like a bullet fired from a .44 magnum, all because we haven't dealt with old wounds!

In movie terms, the ring of power (Lord of the Rings) has influence over us until it is taken back to Mordor and thrown into the fires of Mt. Doom! We have to deal with old offenses in order get our "now issues" in order.

I wonder if we desensitize our thinking when we stay in conflict all the time? Is somebody or something out to get you, hurt you, or wound you at every corner? Really? Could the real problem be that you're wearing your bitterness around your neck, thus creating a shortage of grace when people get around you?

It might be time to prune a few branches on your own tree.

Forgive! Forgive! Forgive!

In the Pages

Does a bad thing in your past easily surface in your conversations when you are upset? Do you remind those you struggle with of their past failures towards you? How quick are you to spew bile, bitterness, and defilement? Why?

Swordplay

November 27
Proverbs 27

"As iron sharpens iron, so one man sharpens another." Proverbs 27:17, NIV

This may be my favorite verse in all of Proverbs. My mind goes straight to all kinds of warrior imagery. If you've seen the movie, *The Kingdom of Heaven*, you have an idea of just how romantically I look at it.

Lord Godfrey (Liam Neeson) commands his son Balian of Ibelin (Orlando Bloom) to grab a sword so he can measure his fighting skills. The monk, concerned that Balian had been riding all night and was probably fatigued, suggests they measure his strength another time. Lord Godfrey responds, *"I once fought two days with an arrow through my testicle. Stand up."*

You get the picture. One has to hone his skills and techniques with those who are better than he is. A brown belt must combat a black belt in order to improve and move up in rank. Surgeons develop surgeons. Chemists teach chemists. Warriors give way to warriors. *Iron sharpens iron.*

This passage is applicable to every one of us, male and female alike. It's not gender specific. We are sharpened by the strong voices and the intense passions of our friends, family, mentors, and anyone else who is willing to invest in us.

It encourages us to call each other out, especially when we see each other drifting towards weakness, danger, or self-pity.

This is the heart of accountability... the combustible element of covenant and community.

We might think the benefit of community is having people to take up the slack when you're not at your best. But it's so much more than that! Think of real community as the greater source of strength that calls my own strengths into more strength.

Yes, it exposes my weaknesses, but it also exercises and strengthens those weaknesses into greatness. The purpose isn't to stay in our comfort zone but to move out into brilliant mystery.

It's not just our fighting skills at stake. The Hebrew implies it's also the sharpening of one's face. That suggests the altering of countenance and character, even personality.

We need this kind of sparring in our lives!

We need people who love us enough to tell us the truth about ourselves. We should want people like that in our lives!

We need brothers and sisters who unselfishly want to see us walk in more anointing and blessing. That's how we become a people who are willing to dig deeper, go harder, and endure longer!

I need my wife to call me out! I need strong men and women to demand more from me. I need it!

Then, when the real battle rages, they come with swords drawn, ready to do battle on my behalf. I can trust them because I have trained with them; I know their commitment to me.

What could be better? What is more honorable?

In The Pages

Who is calling you out right now? Who are you calling out? Describe the value of this kind of swordplay. Is "making you uncomfortable" on the list?

Perils of Usury

November 28
Proverbs 28

"He who increases his wealth by interest and usury gathers it for him who is gracious to the poor." Proverbs 28:8, NASB
I'm all about the Father's love! But I've got a feeling God gets a little grumpy with those of us who have so much and respond so little to the needs of the people around us.

In Proverbs, we get the sense that the Lord pays attention to our money transactions, especially when it comes to the poor. The Law had some very stringent rules about not charging interest to the poor (Ex. 22:25; Lev. 25:36;

Deut. 23:20). You were to help them—not charge them commissions and exorbitant interest.

Today's proverb warns if you take advantage of those who are less fortunate and dependent upon your business and financial expertise, especially the poor, you are sealing the transfer of your wealth to those very people you took advantage of.

Why?

Because God is directly involved in these kinds of transactions. Just because you have money in your pocket today doesn't mean He won't take it away tomorrow.

I used to be a mortgage broker. It took me a while to figure out the business and how to make the transactions work. But once it clicked, I was pretty good at it.

I enjoyed serving my clients and the realtors I worked with. Unfortunately, there was a lot of room for corruption in that industry. We were given quite a bit of freedom. The temptations were everywhere!

You could sell a loan to a client and charge loan fees, underwriting fees, administrative fees, and fees that are sometimes called junk fees. Those junk fees aren't really legitimate, but it adds to the profit margins for the broker.

What most clients failed to realize was how much money is made on the backside for the broker when selling the interest rate. That is where the real money is made in commissions.

One might accept a certain interest rate that is higher than what can actually be bought, only because the bank or broker is being paid to sell a higher rate. Lower income individuals who might not have a great credit score tend to get ripped off in these mortgage transactions, all because they are defenseless and have no other options to secure a better deal.

Early on in my work with clients, I was so hungry to close deals—I literally gave loans away. But later, when the pipeline was full of clients, I had to face this usury temptation everyday.

God would whisper to me: *"Is it fair? Is it right? Mike, what is more important, your peace and integrity, or an extra thousand dollars?"* Usually the only way for me to settle the issue was to put myself in the other person's shoes. Technically, I needed the money, but how would I want to be treated in that kind of a transaction?

Heed Wisdom's warning here. It's not always as easy to make the right choice as you think it will be. There is too much to gain personally. You'll have to fight with those voices that tell you to go the other direction.

In The Pages

What is the difference between usury and profit? Why do you think God put usury regulations into the Law? What would have been Jesus' take on this discussion?

Get Low

November 29
Proverbs 29

"The righteous considers the cause of the poor, but the wicked does not understand such knowledge." Proverbs 29:7, NKJV

"How blessed is the one who treats the poor properly! When trouble comes, the Lord delivers him." Psalms 41:1, NET

Yesterday we looked at the problem of usury towards the poor. Wisdom promises a transfer of our personal wealth to the poor if we choose this kind of exploitation. Today's focus verses encourage us to take action when it comes to the impoverished and indigent.

It's our responsibility to see the poor through the same eyes God sees them with. Because of His influence in our lives, we feel for their circumstances, we share their burdens, and we do what we can with what we have to ease their afflictions.

"The good-hearted understand what it is like to be poor..."
(Proverbs 29:7, MSG).

According to the Hebrew, *"understand"* means so much more than sympathizing with a person who is hungry. It's having serious insight into the overall stress they feel on a daily basis, their never getting ahead—always having to fight to survive.

Our culture is so affluent and wealthy! Those below the poverty line must feel absolutely worthless in comparison. God's people have to be aware of this kind of despair inside the hearts of our brothers and sisters.

According to today's proverb, we have to be much more than aware. We need to be active in serving those who need our help!

In Luke 16:14-31, Jesus confronts the Pharisees. Dr. Luke paints these religious scoffers as *"lovers of money."* It's another one of those passages that remind us that God sees our heart.

We can talk, prance, strut, and declare all we want, but He knows the deep truths inside us. This is where we meet Lazarus, who was so impoverished; he was unable to take care of himself. He was sick, relegated only to the devices of the dogs as they came to lick his sores. Then we learn about the rich man, who lived in luxury and splendor.

Here are two different men who experienced two very different outcomes to their lives. Let's look at it in context.

Poor people were everywhere! Beggars took up station at every intersection. This rich man probably saw Lazarus on a regular basis. The rich man later found himself in torment not because he was rich, but because he had not concerned himself with the hardships of Lazarus. He was totally void of experiential knowledge of his brother's despair. He lived a lifestyle that served self first.

That's what today's lesson is all about. We need to see the needs all around us. We have to!

Psalms says God will bless us when we do. But that blessing can't be the motivation. *"Christ in me"* is our great mover!

In The Pages

How insulated are you from the plight of the poor? What kind of help have you offered in the past? How effective was your effort?

I Said—God Said

November 30
Proverbs 30

"Every word of God is pure: he is a shield unto them that put their trust in him. Add thou not unto his words, lest he reprove thee, and thou be found a liar." Proverbs 30:5-6, KJV

"The believer replied, "Every promise of God proves true; he protects everyone who runs to him for help. So don't second-guess him; he might take you to task and show up your lies." Proverbs 30:5-6, MSG

There are a couple of things I want to point out in these two verses. The original Hebrew for *"word"* in these text is **imrâh** (pronounced *im-ra'*), which implies *the commandment, suggestions, instructions, and speech from God.*

Of course it's pure and good! Whether it comes from the written Word of God (logos) or it's a spoken utterance from Him (rhema)—if He said it, it can be very beneficial to our lives.

Wisdom assures us we can put our trust in Him: He is a *"shield,"* the defender of those who put their trust in Him. God has spoken, God is speaking, and He will continue to speak until the end of time.

Although it's great that so many of us are ready and willing to hear His voice and obey, I wonder if we put more trust in His *"word,"* than we actually put in Him? I've touched on this repeatedly throughout these devotionals.

My devotion to my bible, prophecy, or preaching, doesn't necessarily mean I'm placing my trust in Him. We have this knee-jerk reaction of grabbing our bibles to validate our points. Believe me, I get it. I know what it means to protect and defend myself by quoting my favorite passages. But I wonder if all that exercising of spiritual muscle would be totally necessary if I just surrendered myself to the care, custody, and control of God.

Not the Church, not the Book, not my pastor, not a theology, not another revelation (that's not really new) **. . . just HIM.**

Yeah, it sounds scandalous, but my question stands.

The second thing I want to discuss is how Wisdom instructs us not to add to His words. Most people see this as a warning not to add on to scripture, inserting words, sentences, or whole pages to make it say what you want it to say. Yeah, don't do that!

But what about this: Have you ever been talking with someone who has just made a huge, life-altering decision that doesn't really sound a whole lot like God, only to have them tell you: *"That is what God said"*?

I've lived in spiritual community long enough to have heard just about everything. I've heard people say the words, *"God told me,"* 15-20 times in a matter of 10 minutes! I don't have to be sold on the fact that God talks! But too often we've made up our minds before we take the time to hear God, and then we use the words *"God said"* to end the discussion altogether, before anyone else can offer input or ask any questions.

Honestly, half of the crap we infer *God said,* He didn't say at all.

WE said it.

And we tell ourselves (and everybody else), *"God said it,"* because we want to feel validated and justified in doing what we want to do. But I'll let you in on a little secret. God will pretty much let you do whatever you want to do, so there's really no need to throw Him under the bus to make us feel better.

This is what Wisdom is talking about. Don't do that!

In The Pages

Are you guilty of any of this? Did you hear Him correctly every time? Is there any chance you may have heard incorrectly? I think this is a humility or rejection issue. What do you think I mean by that? What safeguards are built into your hearing and in your actions?

Advent

December 1

The western commercialization of Christmas absolutely wears me out. I really dig the family stuff; the exchanging of gifts among loved ones, and even the decorations and fun traditions. But the excess and over-the-top spending throughout the entire season, followed by those few brief moments on Christmas Eve and Christmas Day where we actually focus on the birth of the Christ, leaves me feeling very sad and restless.

There's just so much going on during the holidays, I wonder if we ever slow down enough to remember what the fuss is really all about.

Today I would like to share an Advent Prayer taken from Friar Richard Rohr's tape series: *Preparing for Christmas*.[15] The word "advent" means the arrival of a notable **person**—not what we've made it into, the arrival of a notable *season*. The poetry in this prayer is beautiful, and the truth is rich. Maybe this can be the year we push in deeper to the Christ. O come, O come, Emmanuel! Let's put our focus and our spirits back on the magnificent truth that He came. And He still comes for us, every day!

O Wisdom, O holy Word of God, you govern all creation with your strong yet tender care. Come, O Sacred Lord of ancient Israel, you showed yourself to Moses in the burning bush and you gave the holy law on Mount Sinai: Come, O Flower of Jesse's stem, you have been raised up as a sign for all peoples; kings stand silent in your presence; the nations bow down in worship before you; Come, O Key of David, O royal Power of Israel, you [not the systems of this world] control at your will the gate of heaven: Come break down the prison walls of death, O Radiant Dawn, splendor of eternal light, sun of justice: Come shine on those who dwell in the darkness and the shadow of death. O, King of all the nations, the only joy of every human heart; O Keystone of the mighty arch of humankind: Come and save these creatures you fashioned from the dust. O, Emmanuel, God-With-Us, king and lawgiver, desire of the nations, Savior of all people: Come and set us free. The Spirit and the bride say, "Come." Amen.

So Mary gives birth to the child. Shepherds nearby receive a visitation from the angel of the Lord. He scares the bejeebers out of them, but they manage to gather themselves to hear his message:

"Don't be afraid. I'm here to announce a great and joyful event that is meant for everybody, worldwide: A Savior has just been born in David's town, a

Savior who is Messiah and Master. This is what you're to look for: a baby wrapped in a blanket and lying in a manger" (Luke 2:10-12, MSG)

Can we dial it down long enough to go back to the manger, to whisper softly and peek into those warm blankets to see the mysterious miracle all over again? May this advent season be the richest, most memorable ever! He has come! Let the earth rejoice! He has come!

In The Pages

What goals have you set for yourself in order to be "a gift" to those around you this Christmas season? Who can you start with today?

Getting Strange

December 2
Proverbs 2

"To deliver you from the strange woman, from the adulteress who flatters with her words" Proverbs 2:16, NASB

Again, we are cautioned in Proverbs 2 to seek wisdom. We find this discourse divided into three parts:

Verses 1-9 say that if we pursue Jehovah God, He will protect us and guard our paths. He has something to say to us about our life cover.

Verses 10-19 show us all the good things that come from heeding the voice of the Lord, verses the terrible things that come to those who don't.

Verses 20-22 encourage us to continue in the way of righteousness to stake our claim in His Kingdom and warn us that taking a different path means being cut off from that inheritance altogether.

Today's focus verse jumped out at me in a way I wasn't quite expecting. I heard myself asking, why? Why is it so taboo (other than the fact that God says so) for men and women to co-mingle their sexual relationships while one or both are married or in committed relationships? Why is infidelity so wrong? How can something so exhilarating, passionate, and romantically motivated be so absolutely destructive and complicated?

I'm going to bypass the textual specifics and move into my pastor-counselor mode. The *"strange woman"* part is what got me thinking about all of this.

Sexuality with the *"strange"* (woman or man) is nothing more than masturbation while using the other person as an object for our satisfaction.

Before the act of sex can be considered "lovemaking," the levels of intimacy in the relationship have to develop past something casual into the realms of love and covenant. We all generally understand these concepts. Unity of spirit, oneness in covenant, and marital union are a mystical promise from the origins of our genesis.

"And the two shall become one flesh" (Ephesians 5:31, NASB).

But here's the problem with sleeping with whomever you want—whenever you want:

There is a spiritual transaction that takes place when two bodies come together in sexual activity.

Soul's mesh.

It literally binds a couple together in Spirit!

Again, *"And the two shall become one flesh"* (Ephesians 5:31, NASB).

A part of your real "self" (your spirit-self or eternal-self) is designed to be wholly given to one mate.

When you give yourself over to more than one person, its like you've given away a piece of the pie; and what you have left over is only a part of what was once whole.

Your spirit was built for one consummation. Thus, your sexual union with someone other than your partner results in a soul-tie with that person. That's a good thing if it's with your mate. It can be problematic if it's only a casual acquaintance.

The bigger problem with a non-marital soul-tie is that you continue to have "relations" in the spirit with that person. It's hard to make a marriage work when one or both partners are tied in the spirit to another person. It's like a "threesome" or "foursome" in a two-person partnership.

Within a sacred covenantal relationship, that soul-tie is absolute and total goodness! It's right! It's part of what sticks and holds you together through thick and thin. And the lovemaking is supposed to be incredible! That was HIS intention all along!

But sex with a stranger is just bad voodoo. There's no way around it!

In The Pages

Are you offended by God's "Do not" or do you ask real questions about why He laid out those instructions? How often does "Because the Bible says so" work for you? What natural problems come from some of these bad choices?

Hounding the Neighbors

December 3
Proverbs 3

"Do not devise harm against your neighbor, while he lives securely beside you." Proverbs 3:29, NASB

I've actually lost count of how many times I've seen *A Christmas Story*. Some years, it's just a couple of times during the holiday season. There are so many great scenes that absolutely crack me up!

One of my favorites is at the end of the movie, when the hillbilly neighbors' bloodhounds tear through the Parker's kitchen, annihilating their specially prepared Christmas turkey. It's total chaos! In an incensed, wild-eyed rage, Ralphie's dad yells out the back door, *"Sonsabitches, Bumpuses!"* So much for peace on earth and goodwill towards men, especially with the Bumpuses as neighbors!

Today's advice is a bit more serious. The word for *"devise"* is **chârash** (pronounced *khaw-rash'*), and it means *"to scratch, to engrave, plough; the use of a tool to fabricate and craft."* Figuratively, *devise* is used here in a negative sense. There is also an implied *"secrecy, silence, and to let alone, or to be deaf to need."* All of this should speak volumes to us!

Seriously, I do realize this is like preaching to the choir. I mostly assume that mature people who walk with God are not out looking for trouble or contention with their neighbors. It would seem a silly notion to suspect otherwise.

But frankly, we need to be careful about intentional and unintentional instigations that could cause tension. Having some awareness of who your neighbors are, and actually being intentional about getting to know them, really does go a long way.

So, do we need to be more sensitive?

Could it be that your beer bottle collection hanging on the dead tree in your front yard doesn't edify your neighbor's love for the neighborhood or endear them to you? What about that '54 coupe that's been under a tarp in your driveway for the last 15 years? Sure, it's your driveway, but are you aware of what your neighbors might think about that rust pile? Have you asked them?

What about your animals? Do they crap in your neighbors' yard, or bark, oink, bleat, or crow incessantly from yours? Eeeeck! It can be so damn irritating to people who don't own pets.

When we turn a deaf ear to the people around us and just do what we want to do, we could be creating a problem.

In America, we think that because we own, we have the right to do whatever we want. This is a self-centered focus, contrary to Kingdom dynamics. Maybe it's time to clean up our sides of the street, our yards, or even more difficult, our attitudes about our freedoms.

In The Pages

How well do you know your neighbors? What are their biggest challenges in life? How do they feel about your community? When was the last time you served them just because you can and want to?

Momma Got Back

December 4
Proverbs 4

"Never walk away from Wisdom—she guards your life; love her—she keeps her eye on you. Above all and before all, do this: Get Wisdom! Write this at the top of your list: Get Understanding! Throw your arms around her—believe me, you won't regret it; never let her go—she'll make your life glorious. She'll

garland your life with grace, she'll festoon your days with beauty." Proverbs 4:5-9, MSG

I've heard it said many times: our view of Father God is deciphered through the eyes of our experiences (or lack thereof) with our natural fathers. It's supposed to be our first encounter with strength beyond our own, protection, and unconditional love. Our relationships with our fathers really do steer our paradigms about how God relates and responds to us.

When I read today's passage, I see David, King of Israel, the warrior, poetic prophet, mighty man, supreme ruler of God's chosen, sitting beside a warm fire with his beloved Solomon, all wide-eyed, nestled in the arms of this larger-than-life man who happens to also be his dad.

David knew God; he had seen God's deliverance many times. His relationship with God was unparalleled. No one even came close! He wasn't afraid of God's presence; he walked in complete freedom. But, even though he walked with God in places that even some priests wouldn't dare to go, he hadn't forgotten any of the mistakes he had made along the way.

As David looks into the black eyes of his adoring son and cradles the thick mop of curly black hair, and then he whispers to him the deepest truths of wisdom. It was truly a real, yet rare Instagram moment.

Nearby, within earshot, sitting in the midst of flickering shadows that play on a nearby wall, is the boy's mother. Bathsheba listens to this exchange between the two special guys in her life. I wonder if she knew David would use her to instill a deep desire within their son for wisdom.

In all of David's royalty, experience, and stature, the best move he ever made was to personify Wisdom as a strong and loving mother.

I can see David glance over and make eye contact with Bathsheba before he says to their son,

"she guards your life, love her...throw your arms around her...never let her go...she'll make your life glorious!"

It makes perfect sense! For the most part, we get that mom is our biggest advocate and promoter. It's written in their DNA. They'll do just about anything for their kids, and it's a very rare anomaly when a mother isn't like this. There is something very... mmmmm... "off" with a mother who chooses herself over the welfare of her children.

In Richard Rohr's book, *Adams Return: The Five Promises of Male Initiation*[16], he tells the story of his time as a chaplain in the prison system. He was shocked to discover that he couldn't seem to keep enough Mother's Day cards in stock for the inmates. But just the opposite was true for Father's Day—no takers for cards for dear ole dad. Even in that environment, it says a great deal about how much of our heart health is tied to our mothers.

David demonstrated his own wisdom in making that connection for Solomon (Proverbs 4:3). Wisdom is like your vested mother. Treat her well, honor her, pay attention to her words, and she'll take care of you!

In The Pages

Was your mother "dialed in" to her children? What part of today's text would confirm your mother's actions towards you? How have you shown your gratitude for her efforts and energies?

My Cistern

December 5
Proverbs 5

"Drink water from your own cistern, running water from your own well. Should your springs overflow in the streets, your streams of water in the public squares? Let them be yours alone, never to be shared with strangers. May your fountain be blessed, and may you rejoice in the wife of your youth. A loving doe, a graceful deer— may her breasts satisfy you always, may you ever be captivated by her love. Why be captivated, my son, by an adulteress? Why embrace the bosom of another man's wife?" Proverbs 5:15-20, NIV

Bring it, Solomon! Woo hoooo! This is not an advertisement for Ozarka water, folks! This man is talking about the amazing and expansive gift of sexuality between a husband and his wife! Much like the metaphors he uses in his Song, the King is bringing a release of Kingdom pleasure for the sanctified union of his subjects.

Let the congregation say, "AMEN!"

For those of you who are married, Wisdom is reminding us that God takes a serious interest in our sex lives with our mates. He designed it to be a source of pleasure and a sense of security. It is to be absent of control, bargaining, and leverage. We are free to pursue each other romantically, to develop intimate connections, and to explore one another completely.

Let me just say, God is a magnificent genius!

To look elsewhere for this kind of true intimacy is stupid and idiotic folly. To those of you who are not yet married, this is a level of sexual meshing that goes way beyond anything you could ever imagine or hope for.

Maybe you've already had a sexual experience outside of marriage. But anything other than the magic that happens in marital sexuality pales in comparison. You haven't really made love until you've experienced this kind of intimacy with your spouse. Don't kid yourself for a minute!

The church is too frikk'n squeamish about this stuff.

As strange as it sounds, I think we've become so preoccupied with finding the perfect spiritual connection with a potential partner, we've forgotten some of the plain ole natural dynamics between a man and a woman. No marriage is perfect. You're going to face problems together, no matter how deep a spiritual connection you have.

Patti and I counsel a lot of young adults in search of their future spouses. Of course we don't promote promiscuity or illicit lustful behavior, but geez, it's okay for a guy to notice that a woman has curves! Adam saw and he liked. It is okay for a young woman to notice the natural strength of a man! God put those kinds of desires in us for a purpose.

It is called *sex appeal*, and it's not a sin to choose a spouse you are sexually attracted to. Actually, it's quite necessary.

Trust me, God will take care of the spiritual growth between the two of you if you'll both dedicate yourselves to Him. If you do that, He'll bless your sexual relationship and all other aspects of your marriage.

It makes the days much brighter and the nights all the more exciting!

In The Pages

When is the last time you thanked your mate for all the gifts they are to you? If married, what stands in the way of your sexual freedom? If single, what potential benefits do you see in the fidelity of marital sexuality?

Anti-venom

December 6
Proverbs 6

"These six things the Lord hates, yes, seven are an abomination to Him: a proud look, a lying tongue, hands that shed innocent blood, a heart that devises wicked plans, feet that are swift in running to evil, a false witness who speaks lies, and one who sows discord among brethren." Proverbs 6:16-19, NKJ

"Here are six things God hates, and one more that he loathes with a passion..." Proverbs 6:16, MSG

So here is a creative style of writing. It's a system known as the (X+1) formula, or pattern, depending on which commentary you're looking at. It was a way to present items that were not to be a complete or exhaustive list. The idea was to bundle the list, with emphasis on the last item added to that list.

So here, the first six items are to be looked at and dealt with individually, but the crux of the message is that seventh item. That's the heart of the message, the Lord's heart.

The word *"hate"* is **sânê'** (pronounced *saw-nay'*), which means *"a personal hate."* So, it's a *personal* thing to the Lord. All of these things listed are *personally* offensive to Him.

It messes with me when I realize there are things we do that actually wound the Lord.

We figure He's strong enough to handle all the crap in this world. It doesn't often dawn on us that He is also very tenderhearted and personally vested in our lives. Even once I recognize my sin, repent, and fall at His feet with remorse, I figure God just deals with it. Guess we need to tap into the fact that He actually feels this stuff too.

"Bless those who curse you, pray for those who mistreat you"
(Luke 6:28, NASB).

Rather than focus on these negatives, let me give you the counter actions that bring Kingdom whenever you encounter some of the stuff mentioned above. These are things God personally loves:

A real and humble spirit,

A truth talker (no embellishments, no exaggerations),

A protector and advocate of those who cannot
(or will not) defend themselves,

A heart that dwells on and seeks the good in everything and everyone,

Feet that walk down righteous paths,

A conscience that chooses to honor, no matter what the outcome
or who notices.

The mere presence of someone who possesses all of these traits commands the blessing of unity and agreement in the Body of Christ! It is so good and so right that God can't help Himself, and He commands a manifest blessing (see Psalms 133).

This is getting to the real desire in His heart!

In The Pages

Is it easier to go through life trying to correct the mistakes we've made in the past, or is it better to go forward with a notion of what God likes and loves? What areas do you need to work on? Ask for His help. He's into this stuff.

Shikolahsikotakadebeda!

December 7
Proverbs 7

"And I saw among the naive, and discerned among the youths a young man lacking sense. " Proverbs 7:7, NASB

"Therefore let him who thinks he stands take heed lest he fall. No temptation has overtaken you except such as is common to man; but God is faithful, who will not allow you to be tempted beyond what you are able, but with the temptation will also make the way of escape, that you may be able to bear it." 1 Corinthians 10:12-13, NASB

I believe this passage in 1 Corinthians 10. God has been faithful to give me the strength and patience to bear and overcome some very hard situations, or else He gave me a way of escape.

The Holy Spirit can be so present when we need Him!

Not that I've always made the right choices or came out on top, but the fact that God has always been in the whirlwind with me is comforting. It reassures me that He sees and hears us. Many years of practical experience have solidified my confidence in this promise.

The context today is the key. Proverbs 7:22 says a young man who lacks sense follows after his temptress *"as an ox goes to the slaughter."* I get chills up and down my spine! But not because of what happens! You sleep with the dogs—you rise with fleas. I get all that.

What is disturbing to me is that these young men (or women) are unaware of how much danger they are actually in. An ox is totally unaware that he is about to be slaughtered. Not a clue!

When we hear the word *"naïve,"* we think young, innocent, gullible, sheltered, and maybe even overprotected. In reality, the word **pᵉthâ'îy** (pronounced *peth-aw-ee'*) is a lot harsher.

Think in terms of *"stupid, foolish, and willing to be seduced."* Maybe not brave enough to venture out on their own, but willing to be carried away if the right-offer comes along.

People like this are "easy pickings" for a professional bloodsucker. What's even more disturbing, these are sons and daughters who fall prey to such casualties! These aren't just nameless, faceless statistics, but actual carriers of genetic and spiritual code—created for a high purpose!

Lady Wisdom describes these young individuals as *"lacking sense."* The word is **lêb** (pronounced *labe*), which means, *"heart."* These youth are lacking *heart*, which is the center of intellect, emotion, desire, passion, and purpose. There is no fire in them to drive them to greatness. They can't see past what is there in front of them.

Wisdom is crying (and I cry along with her!) with every fiber of Her being:

"SON, BEAUTIFUL DAUGHTER, YOU ARE BETTER THAN THIS!

TO HELL WITH THE DEVIL! RUN! GET A GRIP!

DO NOT SETTLE FOR LESS THAN THE GREATNESS INSIDE OF YOU!"

In The Pages

Forget journaling today! Pray with your mind, pray in the Spirit, cry out for your destiny, and plead that your heart be satisfied! God loves this stuff! Go for it!

Fusion

December 8
Proverbs 8

*"The Lord **possessed** me at the beginning of His way, before His works of old."* Proverbs 8:22, NKJ

*"The Lord **created** me as the beginning of his works, before his deeds of long ago."* Proverbs 8:22, NET

Proverbs 8:22-31 is generally recognized as the most obvious reference to Jesus Christ in all of Proverbs. Nothing in the text specifically names him. But at the same time, all of it could easily be referring to Jesus. This is the stuff that makes theologians smile.

There are two roots for the Hebrew **qânâh** (pronounced *kaw-naw'*), which can be interpreted, *"possessed"* or *"created."* I've highlighted both of these words above. Some scholars believe Christ is the revelation of God's wisdom, so we're going to apply that concept here.

*"For indeed Jews ask for signs and Greeks search for wisdom; but we preach Christ crucified, to Jews a stumbling block and to Gentiles foolishness, but to those who are the called, both Jews and Greeks, **Christ the power of God and the wisdom of God**"* (1 Corinthians 1:22-24, NASB).

*"For I want you to know how great a struggle I have on your behalf and for those who are at Laodicea, and for all those who have not personally seen my face, that their hearts may be encouraged, having been knit together in love, and attaining to all the wealth that comes from the full assurance of understanding, resulting in a true knowledge of God's mystery, **that is, Christ***

Himself, in whom are hidden all the treasures of wisdom and knowledge" (Colossians 2:1-3, NASB).

My question today is simple: what are we doing with Wisdom? If it's true what these theologians say, what are we doing with this Christ?

Did God give us Wisdom? Did He give us Christ only for our own personal benefit, or do we have a responsibility to share this good news with others? I was reminded this morning that God shared himself with us. Christ came for us. God became manifest for us, so as to leave no doubt what love actually looks like.

It's not enough that God came (past tense). God still comes every single day! And we are the bearers, the fingers of His touch—the voice of His truth!

Living and sharing Wisdom's work includes the heart and life of Christ. It has always included Christ.

In The Pages

Read Proverbs 8:22-31. What else did you hear the Lord speak to you today about the fusion of Wisdom and Christ? Do you prefer *"possessed"* or *"created?"* Why?

Wine, Bread, Meat

December 9
Proverbs 9

"Come, eat my food and drink the wine I have mixed. Leave your simple ways and you will live; walk in the way of understanding." Proverbs 9:5-6, NIV

Proof texting is when a person appeals to a biblical text to prove or justify a theological position without regard for the context of the passage they are citing. When I look at this verse, it reminds me just how easy it is to proof text with the Bible. Without context, it's easy to pick out our favorite passages and apply them to whatever point we're trying to make.

When I read the words, *"Come eat, drink the wine I have mixed,"* I think, "Oh boy, here we go again!" Voices of irresponsibility and folly will interpret this verse to say, *"See, God wants us to get hammered!"*

On the flip side of the coin, religious devils will manipulate the scripture to argue it's not really talking about actual wine. Why? *"Because wine is bad."* That's not right either.

What Lady Wisdom is offering us here is good food, rest, laughter, joy, fellowship, and yes, good wine! But remember that whoever prepares the spread has some authority over the overall benefits of what we ingest. As she offers us these things, she's hoping we'll take away with us community, moderation, honor, integrity, and proper accountability.

"Ho! Every one who thirsts, come to the waters; and you who have no money come, buy and eat. Come, buy wine and milk without money and without cost. "Why do you spend money for what is not bread, and your wages for what does not satisfy? Listen carefully to Me, and eat what is good, and delight yourself in abundance. Incline your ear and come to Me. Listen, that you may live; and I will make an everlasting covenant with you, according to the faithful mercies shown to David" (Isaiah 55:1-3, NASB).

"'I am the Bread—living Bread!—who came down out of heaven. Anyone who eats this Bread will live—and forever! The Bread that I present to the world so that it can eat and live is myself, this flesh-and-blood self.' At this, the Jews started fighting among themselves: "How can this man serve up his flesh for a meal?" But Jesus didn't give an inch. 'Only insofar as you eat and drink flesh and blood, the flesh and blood of the Son of Man, do you have life within you. The one who brings a hearty appetite to this eating and drinking has eternal life and will be fit and ready for the Final Day. My flesh is real food and my blood is real drink. By eating my flesh and drinking my blood you enter into me and I into you. In the same way that the fully alive Father sent me here and I live because of him, so the one who makes a meal of me lives because of me. This is the Bread from heaven. Your ancestors ate bread and later died. Whoever eats this Bread will live always'" (John 6:50-58, MSG).

We are in a season of feasting—not fasting. This is the time to celebrate the wholeness of Wisdom and the fullness of our King's influence in our lives.

Eat and drink in honor of what He has done!

Remember why you have liberty, and exercise your freedom, all in the moderation of full honor to our Savior!

In The Pages

Reread those passages above. What happens in your heart when you focus on the delicacies that the Lord has prepared for all who are invited to the table?

Peace

December 10

"And you, child, will be called the prophet of the Most High; for you will go on before the Lord to prepare His ways; to give to His people the knowledge of salvation by the forgiveness of their sins, because of the tender mercy of our God, with which the Sunrise from on high will visit us, to shine upon those who sit in darkness and the shadow of death, to guide our feet into the way of peace" (Luke 1:76-79, NASB).

Back when I was the Senior Pastor of a little church in Texas, I used to pick one Sunday in December to preach out of Luke's gospel. One Sunday. One sermon.

The way we (the Church) typically speed through our Savior's birth story reminds me of a NASCAR pit stop. With tires still smoking; we pull over just long enough to reflect on the "wonder" of Jesus Christ in a fleeting moment of time we call Christmas. I'm trying my best to avoid a tirade against the American commercialization of Christmas. I just want us to remember what Christmas is really all about, and to keep that memory sacred in our hearts.

"... *to guide our feet into the way of peace" (Luke 1:79, NASB)*

Oh, how I love those words! If we can just keep these words in our hearts and in our spirits, they will take us to another place altogether.

Zacharias's prophecy about his son, the one we identify as John the Baptist, is very powerful. Luke tells us that Zacharias was filled with the Holy Spirit, and then he let loose these incredible words of promise and favor on both John and the Christ child.

His word told of future events as they would actually play out. Of all that is packed into those verses, I'm always taken back by the words (sorry, one more time), *"to guide our feet into the way of peace."*

This isn't the kind of peace John Lennon sang about, or what antiwar activists march for. Any peace that is dependent upon the actions of our government, or humanity in general, in order to maintain that peace, is nothing more than a thin layer of ice, vulnerable to crack under the slightest pressure. Think about it. Even with all the nuclear weaponry in this world, which is supposedly "keeping the peace," there's still global conflict.

We've seen racism, civil war, even genocide—all rooted in deep-seeded hate. International governments staff thousands upon thousands of people to maneuver and manipulate diplomacy, or at least the semblance of diplomatic unity.

NO! Zacharias is talking about a peace that comes from another source. It's a place of true internal rest, acquired only by the influence of the Prince of Peace Himself.

True personal peace can be achieved easily enough through our knowing Jesus. It's maintaining that peace that requires a little more attention on our parts.

Ultimately, it's about our decrease, and His increase.

These things will continue to develop in our lifelong love affair with the Lord.

The longer I walk with my wife, the more I love her; the better I love her. Covenant builds a desire in our hearts to serve what He served and love what He loved. That within itself releases a part of the peace that we are promised by Zacharias.

In The Pages

What is better than internal and external peace? What areas are lacking His peace in your life? Who else do you know who needs this kind of peace in his or her life?

Trickle Down

December 11
Proverbs 11

"He who brings trouble on his family will inherit only wind, and the fool will be servant to the wise." Proverbs 11:29, NIV

"Exploit or abuse your family, and end up with a fistful of air; common sense tells you it's a stupid way to live." Proverbs 11:29, MSG

This verse is the last of three verses teaching on the misuse of wealth in Proverbs 11. I think Peterson has caught the real heart of Wisdom here. When a person whose heart is right makes a financial mistake, it may cause a setback, but the family is still intact. But when that person's heart isn't right, he and his entire family get wind—lots and lots of wind!

Let's take a closer look at the word *"wind."* The Hebrew is **rûwach** (pronounced *roo'-akh*), and it means, *"to breathe the exhalation of life and anger."* It also means *"empty air."*

Today's focus verse is steeped in the basic concept of sowing and reaping. If you sow trouble into your family, you reap angry wind and empty air, which is tied directly to your inheritance. In other words, your negative actions have the potential to disqualify you from the "inheritance" of goods.

This was a big deal back in the day, especially among children. Each kid knew his place in the birth order and what he stood to inherit. Bringing dishonor to his parents had serious consequences. It was a big deal to lose your inheritance.

Inheritance is not just limited to money or material goods. There is a very important spiritual dynamic that takes place within a family, where what happens at the top flows down to the bottom.

One might use the words: trickle down.

People make crazy choices sometimes that really defy sound logic and common sense. Call it a bad decision, even stupidity. I've done it, you've done it – we all make mistakes. But how often do we acknowledge the spiritual consequences of some of those poor choices, especially when they affect the people closest to us?

Parents: the heavy hand of dead religion forced upon a family unit is a pretty substantial invitation for those kids to act out in rebellion in the future. We then look at the rebellion as the issue, failing to recognize the role we played in causing some of that rebellion in the first place. Some kids will comply as long as they are under your roof, but once they are out on their own, they aim for destruction of any and all barriers! Not good!

What happens when a parent allows abuse in the home? Statistically, people who are abused as kids are more likely to become abusers themselves without some serious spiritual help. If a home is governed with violence and rage, then we can expect some devastating collateral damage! Be mindful of what seeds you are planting at home, because come harvest time, you may end up with fruit you don't really want.

In The Pages

Today, listen to Harry Chapin's song, *Cats in the Cradle*. What was the "trickle down" in that song? What is the overall message of the song?

Tell Me I Suck

December 12
Proverbs 12

"Whoever loves discipline loves knowledge, but he who hates correction is stupid." Proverbs 12:1, NIV

"If you love learning, you love the discipline that goes with it—how shortsighted to refuse correction!" Proverbs 12:1, MSG

There are 10 chapters in Proverbs that use this variation of the word "*discipline*." Here it's **mûwçâr** (pronounced *moo-sawr´*) meaning, *"bond of restraint, correction, an educating rebuke."*

My dad was my first larger-than-life hero. I was always into doing "guy stuff," but with my dad, it was always on another level altogether!

My earliest recollection of hunting was at this little caliche-bottomed creek in Central Texas. My dad and I were waiting patiently at the water's edge for the dove to come in for a cool drink. Even though I wasn't big enough to hold up the 12-gauge shotgun my dad was carrying, I was so anxious to shoot the gun at a real target.

My dad told me the gun was too powerful for such a little guy. But I assured him I was capable and willing. So with him supporting the gun in his hands, he allowed me to shoulder as best as I could, take aim, and pull the trigger. It all happened very fast. Too fast. I do remember a few things about that experience:

First, I thought I had unleashed hell! No, seriously... hell!

Second, the kick from the gun knocked the wind out of me, and I slumped over, making that sick sound distressed frogs make. I thought I was dying!

Third, my dad was laughing his ass off! Then he said, *"Okay, let's try it again, but why don't you let me help you this time?"* I was all ears... this time. With his coaching, I actually shot the gun several more times without it caving-in my skinny little chest. It made all the difference in the world!

There is this young man I've known for about three years now (2011) who really gets the value of today's scripture and has written it on his heart. I don't want to embarrass him, so I'll just call him Champ.

In our spiritual community, we teach that feedback is one of the most necessary dynamics of living in covenantal community. Without regular feedback and honest dialogue, there is just too much room for conflict. We make assumptions based on what we hear. We misunderstand, misinterpret, and misjudge one another. When the system isn't flushed on a regular basis, we fall prey to taking offense and harboring bitterness.

It takes courage to give feedback! It's a demonstration of vital integrity and genuine love.

But the bigger question is: can we *receive* the feedback?

The Champ receives feedback better than anyone I know. It is a rare thing to get around this guy without hearing him asking for, digging for, more corrective feedback from myself or any other person who has oversight in his life.

I know him well enough to know he's not asking for anything sugar-coated. Champ is asking for a kick in the butt! It's not a morbid thing. The guy is aware of the call and anointing on his life. He knows he is accountable for how he presents himself. He understands that he is forming foundations right now for the stuff God will shortly be building in his life.

This meticulous pressing for feedback is the highest form of wisdom a person can display! If we can get our communities to embrace this same attitude and model of self-examination, we'll see an outpouring from the Spirit that will rock the Church!

I say BRING IT!

In The Pages

When is the last time you asked for raw and real feedback from an elder or a peer? Can you take it? Do you want it? Really?

Social Pretense

December 13
Proverbs 13

"There is one who pretends to be rich, but has nothing; another pretends to be poor, but has great wealth. Proverbs 13:7, NASB

At first glance, you think Wisdom is referring to the unwise steward who is continually living above his or her means. Or the more meager person who lives well beneath his or her means, but is actually quite wealthy.

We all know a few old misers like that, still clinging to the first dollar they ever earned. We call them stingy, crusty—unwilling to let go of their money for any reason whatsoever. But what Wisdom is talking about today isn't really about money.

This is a pretense issue. It's about deceit, fraud—a charade. Why pretend?

We see a lot of wannabe rich folks out there; that's fairly common these days. But why pretend to be "better off" than you are? And why pretend to be poor if there is an abundance of wealth? The answer lies in the motivation of a person's heart.

Simply put, if no one thinks you have anything, nothing is usually required of you. If everyone thinks you are poor, no one is asking for a hand out. Today's scripture isn't encouraging modesty. It's confronting deception in order to escape from responsibility. Those who have, like it or not, have some responsibility in the arena of stewardship and benevolence.

When I was in my third pastorate, there was a man on the membership roll who I never saw in church once during my three-year tenure. I made phone calls to his home, but he never returned one of my calls. I made visits to his home, but could never get him to come to the front door. I would see him in town, in various venues, but I could never get the guy to acknowledge my attempts to engage him.

But he had a ritual.

Every day, he made a trip to the bank at 11:00 a.m. and then again at 3:30 p.m. It was a set-your-watch-by-it guarantee. I had friends who worked in the bank, so I inquired about the old bachelor.

He was an only child, heir to a ranching and oil fortune. He went to the bank each day to check the accrued interest on his savings accounts and CDs. The numbers would change in the morning and again in the afternoon, so he was there every day to get the updates.

When you saw him at the local diner, he was always sitting alone at the same table, eating the same food, talking to no one, just pouring over his account balances. That was it! That was his life.

The old timers in town said he had more money than God. His car was trashy and rusted, he was always dressed frumpy and simple, and he looked like he needed benevolence most of the time! How a person can just turn off life like that?

Maybe he got tired of people asking for help, or he got burned in a bad loan situation. Whatever it was, it turned him to silence and fearful solitude. There is no reason to hide, outwardly or inwardly.

God has more for us than that kind of seclusion. We have a chance to steward all of our blessings with favor and thankful order that touches a hurting world.

In The Pages

What is your take on why people pretend in such matters? If you had ten minutes at this guy's lunch table, what would you say to him?

Bitter Roots

December 14
Proverbs 14

"The heart knows its own bitterness, and a stranger does not share its joy."
Proverbs 14:10, NKJV

What a great verse! Let me give you the Central Texas redneck rundown in a single sentence:

"Whether you are living with a burr under your saddle or spilling over back-slapp'n happy, it's hard to explain to someone else why you are the way you are."

Yeah, it's silly, but that is the veneer of it. Surely there is more going on here? How do we get cut from the herd in these two areas and find ourselves so isolated? I'll take the negative first and finish with the positive.

Back on November 26, we discussed how an unhealed heart leads to bitterness. Hebrews 12:14-15 says,

"Pursue peace with all people, and holiness, without which no one will see the Lord: looking carefully lest anyone fall short of the grace of God; lest any root of bitterness springing up cause trouble, and by this many become defiled" (NKJV).

How do so many people become defiled by bitterness?

It's simple. We talk, we gossip, we build alliances, we look for opportunities to share our stories of how we were wronged.

The Greek word for *"bitterness"* is **pikria** (pronounced *pik-ree´-ah*) meaning, *"acridity, poison, or acid."* We know this in the natural as bile.

As gross as it is, this is the perfect picture of how this defilement happens. Someone vomits on you (with their offense, their wound, and their bitterness), and the remnants of that puke (the green bile stuff) will stain your garments when it lands on you.

Now, that will not immediately make you bitter. But if you take up that offense or take up the wound, then bitterness can develop inside of your heart if you do not also forgive.

People don't become bitter because of what happened to them.
They got that way because they refused to forgive.

Proverbs says when we allow our wounds to sit in the cooker for too long, they start to taste bitter. That *bitterness* becomes unique to us, so we isolate ourselves. One more time, you can't make me bitter because you offended me. I make myself bitter because I will not forgive!

In 2006, I had a loving friend tell me that I was blowing my witness (and potentially my future in ministry) with my constant spewing of vile bitterness towards the Church. I had to forgive it all! I had to let go of every offense and all of the pain.

And when I asked HIM to take it from me, all of that pain and bitterness disappeared. My life changed drastically in a very short period of time as soon as I gave all of that up!

I had been in a dead dry desert for a good five years because of my unwillingness to forgive! I had totally isolated myself from the very people God had destined me to reach! Fortunately, He waited patiently for me to come to my senses.

The *joy* part of this is easier. Our source of joy is the Holy Spirit (Galatians 5:22). Again, this is generated deep inside of us.

There is no faking joy. Pious smiles, shallow faith, and exhaustive pretending don't express joy. Joy comes off of you when it's Him and it's real. Joy is infectious and life giving! Your religious "hallelujah" can't touch joy! Seek the source and wear the fruit! You will be in your own little world! That's why people look at you the way they do.

In The Pages

Do you have a wound that you can't stop talking or thinking about? How long before you let Him take that from you? How about right now? Please?

Posers

December 15
Proverbs 15

"God can't stand pious poses, but he delights in genuine prayers. A life frittered away disgusts God; he loves those who run straight for the finish line." Proverbs 15:8-9, MSG

Back in the day when the Old Covenant was totally operational, there was a lot of emphasis on right and wrong, good and evil, life or death. Although we are no longer under the influence of that old law (unless we choose to live under its influence and death sentence), there is still a lot of truth and insight there into God's heart and what He loves about His creation.

Peterson's translation motivates me to ask myself some questions about *"pious poses."* Admittedly, few have been more zealous than I have been in the pursuit of religious activity for external reasons. I'm not proud of this confession, just realistically aware, and willing to acknowledge it.

I wonder if we really ever consider that all of our religious pageantry is actually something that *disgusts God*? It's a life He considers *frittered away*! I know we are prone to religious activity, and sometimes we forget about the heart aspect, but the Lord is very dialed in to our heart condition!

King David pretty much brushed past the mold of old reverence traditions. He knew the warnings God had given the people about ritual without heart (1 Samuel 15:22; Isaiah 1:11; Jeremiah 6:20).

The system they had in place at the time meant a lot of animals were sacrificed in ceremonial worship and sanctifying efforts. David also participated in this system, but he was motivated by the stuff floating around in his heart, not by an unhealthy fear than God wanted to kill him. Even though our current system is totally different, we'd do well to glean what we can out of David's raw walk with God.

David was so freaking human, absolutely vulnerable, bent towards error, and totally exposed in his frailty! He's one of the greatest examples in scripture of what it means to live outside of the religion box.

In 2 Samuel 24, we read the story of David numbering the people. If you can get past the head scratching of the first verse, you'll manage the rest of the story pretty well. In short, 70,000 people die because of David's census. Once the gravity of his fatal error hits David's heart, God instructs David to construct an altar and offer prayers, burnt offerings, and peace offerings, on behalf of the people.

We get a glimpse into David's heart when he refuses to allow Araunah to give him the threshing floor to make his offerings. David was not willing to take a shortcut with God here. The King wasn't sacrificing to keep up an appearance of veneration. David was sacrificing because he was trying to get his heart right with the God he loved.

A cheap top dressing just wasn't an option. David needed to ante up for the place of his sacrifice. None of his worship was infused with piety. This was real brokenness.

In The Pages

Can you worship anywhere with anyone? Does your heart determine your ritual, or do your rituals reveal your heart? Are you sure about that? How important is worship style to you? Is one style better than another?

Bad Paths

December 16
Proverbs 16

"There is a way which seems right to a man, but its end is the way of death."
Proverbs 16:25, NASB

In Romans 1:18-32, the Apostle Paul warns us of some pretty significant consequences that come to those who choose not to exercise faith in God. We don't have time to get into that passage here, but take a moment and read Paul's opinion of Roman culture 2000 years ago. This could have easily been written about our culture today! Read it out of *The Message* and you'll make some easy connections!

With all of our social and technological advances, we still haven't quite been able to develop an external solution to man's internal moral issues. The intellectuals are pretty convinced that anything and everything can be rectified with a formula. I'm sorry, but the seared conscience of the godless and lack of "God fear" from the faithless can't be fixed with a formula.

Many (not all) men and women continue to live outside of faith and apart from the touch of the divine. God still loves us (I really believe that!), so He allows us to go it alone for as long as we see fit. But to deny God's desire for influencing access through any number of avenues is to disallow a very real option for spiritual governance and order in our lives. Wisdom declares that way does not end well for any of us.

All of that is heavy... real heavy if you hang there for very long. So it helps for us to remember that God really loves us—ALL of us! God *IS* love.

But we still have a job to do. It's our responsibility to bring light and to live the good news. We still have the task of allowing the hardest of the hard to see our soft and tender heart!

Yelling at people who don't confess our values that they're going to hell is a waste of time. They know they haven't bought in, and they might like being in that position. Moreover, they're likely to stay that way until they either decide they don't want to be lost anymore or the Holy Spirit draws them into an encounter with the Savior.

I liked my lostness. You probably liked yours too.

I grew up in the church, but by the time I was 20 years old, I wasn't making any decisions according to biblical principle, religious moral code, or any other kind of spiritual influence. I made decisions based on my own selfish interests.

It was what seemed *right to me*, and I made no apologies for where I was at that time. It wasn't until the Holy Spirit started messing with me that I made some serious adjustments about how I was living.

So what do we do with the people we're around, our family and friends, who are out there in their own unbelief system and deep into their own way?

First of all, we don't condemn!

We love them, we pray, we serve them, and we wait for an opportunity to speak words of life. That's it. There is no magic pixie dust.

If you force religion with them... well... you're not helping them.

As a child, I spent three weeks every summer with my sweet Pentecostal grandma in Arkansas. She'd drag me down to the altar every Sunday for the pastor and his wife to lay hands on me. They'd prophesy, pray, and cry out for me! I remember it like it was yesterday!

My faith-filled grandma prayed like a warrior and waited on her God to open my eyes! It took some time, but she finally got her victory!

Don't think for a second that your prayers and service to others are in vain! Nothing is wasted in the Kingdom! Prophesy life! Speak life! Expect life! God will do the rest.

In The Pages

Is any person beyond God's reach? Do you have the patience to wait and the endurance to pursue God's help in the hard cases? Who is on your hard list?

Real Consolation

December 17

"For my eyes have seen Your salvation, Which You have prepared in the presence of all peoples, A LIGHT OF REVELATION TO THE GENTILES, And the glory of Your people Israel." Luke 2:30-32, NASB

I wonder why Christmastime has such a strange hold over us. I mean we spend about 30 days totally restructuring our lives around Christmas themes and traditions that produce floods of emotions. I'm not saying any of that is wrong. Sometimes it's great to be around family and friends, eating good food and enjoying each other's company. But are we really being authentic?

Even the Grinch is willing to come around at Christmastime to reconcile a few issues. Why do we only feel obligated to do this at Christmas? It feels forced, disingenuous, and leaves us feeling exhausted. I just want us to see beyond the sea of pretty paper, twinkling lights, and sentimental "Christmas cheer" and be honest with ourselves.

The truth is, some people carry real pain that actually increases during Christmastime! People are lost out there, alone, and hurting deeply.

An old friend recently came into my office, sat down, and cried like a baby. This guy doesn't usually show a lot of outward emotion, but I know his pain rages internally. His teenage daughter died 7 months ago. She won't be at the dinner table this Christmas, or any day thereafter. He's not thinking about what presents he'll get or give this year.

Another buddy used to tell me how the holidays were tormenting for him before he met the Lord. Even genuine acts of love felt like plastic hugs to him, fleeting and impermanent—just another painful reminder that something was missing from his life. There was never enough Old Milwaukee to numb the aching loneliness he felt, even though he lived totally surrounded by people who loved him. He was lost inside.

Only God knows the real intent in our hearts.

But no matter how we treat our lost friends and family during Christmas, there is only one present that will satisfy what mankind really longs for. There is only One who will fill that void in their hearts.

Until they see it, until they receive it, we need to have more grace for where they are now. No one can see in the dark. It doesn't help them for me to cluck my tongue and point out their blindness! Why do we do that? Jesus didn't do that to us.

Even now, when I mess up, Father God doesn't yell at me, cuss me, slap me upside the head, or shame me. He comforts me! Like a father cares for his helpless baby, He cradles me, changes my dirty diaper, bandages my wounds, and accepts me back into the very arms I push so hard to get myself out of!

Who else does that for us?

My behavior may disappoint, discourage, and even disgust others and create all kinds of issues for me to live with, but God receives me right back into His bosom, again… and again…. and again.

My point is this: in a few days, the magical *hold* of Christmas will have lifted once more off of our world. Will I, will you, come out of it feeling empty, exhausted, and broke?

Or will we come out of it fully alive and freshly refilled with the magnificent wonder and awe that God *"came"* for each and every one us? That is a sustaining truth that should rock our worlds 24 hours a day, 365 days a year! Merry Christmas!

In The Pages

Are you consumed with commercialism during the Christmas season, or can you keep the main thing the main thing? How do you get into the Christmas rhythm? What is your favorite spiritual tradition for Christmas?

Give Me Shelter

December 18
Proverbs 18

"The name of the Lord is a strong tower; the righteous runs into it and is safe." Proverbs 18:10, NASB

"God's name is a place of protection—good people can run there and be safe." Proverbs 18:10, MSG

Solomon never sounded more like his dad than when he said stuff like this! Back when David was full of warrior energy, fighting the battles of Israel while dodging King Saul's spears, he would sing mighty songs of God's deliverance. David was prone to making glorious and magnificent declarations of God's help and protection:

"The Lord is my rock and my fortress and my deliverer; my God, my rock, in whom I take refuge, my shield and the horn of my salvation, my stronghold and my refuge; my savior, You save me from violence. I call upon the Lord, who is worthy to be praised, and I am saved from my enemies. For the waves of death encompassed me; the torrents of destruction overwhelmed me; the cords of

Sheol surrounded me; the snares of death confronted me. In my distress I called upon the Lord, yes, I cried to my God; and from His temple He heard my voice, and my cry for help came into His ears" (2 Samuel 22:2-7, NASB).

One of my favorite "old preacher" stories is when David danced naked in the streets of Jerusalem! After being held captive by the Philistines for far too long, the Lord of Hosts was welcomed home.

Overjoyed, David set aside his dignity and religious piety, stripped off his robes, and danced in his birthday suit, as priests swayed along in rhythm with the Ark of the Covenant (the literal presence of God) on their shoulders. What a day of celebration!

Once the party was over and David was again in attire, his first wife, Michal (Saul's daughter), pulled him aside and rebuked his worship. Her condescending tongue-lashing was meant to rob David of his joy and restore honor and dignity to herself and her father. Such poisonous tactics must have wounded David deeply.

The King was a sensitive guy. I'm sure David had to find a place to wash his spirit and clear his mind after such an assault. So he disappeared to his quiet place and safe house, his sanctuary.

After a while, servants began to look for David and security was notified that the king was missing. Joab soon remembered where to look for David, and he and a few men went to the Tabernacle. There, under the golden box, where most dare not enter, lay the king of Israel.

"David, are you alright my lord?" This tiny ball of broken man and shredded heart unfurled and handed a crumpled piece of parchment to one of the soldiers. Inscribed on it was what we now know as Psalm 91. It begins,

"He who dwells in the shelter of the Most High will abide in the shadow of the Almighty. I will say to the Lord, "My refuge and my fortress, my God, in whom I trust!" (NASB).

In the midst of sorrow, David knew where his help, his peace, his comfort, and his healing came from! HIS presence.

In The Pages

Where do you run when it's not good inside of you? How long does it take for you to get there? Who do you tell first, God or other people?

Different Kind Of Robbery

December 19
Proverbs 19

"He who assaults his father and drives his mother away is a shameful and disgraceful son." Proverbs 19:26, NASB

"Oh yeah, Paschall, great Christmas message!" Hang with me. There is more going on in this passage than a brutish adolescent who has been too aggressive with his parents.

The word *"assaults"* is **shâdad** (pronounced *shaw-dad'*), which means, *"to rob or oppress."* Think about it.

How many different things can a parent be robbed of by a child's bad behavior?

What kind of person drives his own mother away? We kind of understand young men who have issues with over-bearing or abusive fathers, but the first touch of nurture and raw love we ever experience is with our mothers!

Wisdom says this behavior is *"disgraceful."* The word **châphêr** (pronounced *khaw-fare'*) suggests a confusion that does not make sense to bystanders. They are left wondering how such behavior could possibly be warranted. Even if your parents are Beelzebub incarnate, doesn't Wisdom suggest another avenue instead of aggression and withholding?

If you're single or married, consider this: what happens when you get along with your parents, but your significant other does not? Wisdom says it is shameful and disgraceful to rob your parents of anything.

Remember, if you are married, you are one with your mate and a rightful part of the family unit. Those are now your parents too. I said earlier, there are a lot of ways to rob your parents: abstaining from family functions, denying them time with their grandchildren, causing turmoil, and stealing peace and joy.

This kind of stuff would break the hearts of most parents!

It can also be upsetting to other family members who are directly or indirectly affected. No one sins unto himself alone. The ripple effects can tear a family apart!

What happens when a widowed, sick, or aging parent needs help and the children refuse to come to their aid? The Apostle Paul said,

"Anyone who neglects to care for family members in need repudiates the faith. That's worse than refusing to believe in the first place" (1 Timothy 5:8, MSG).

In other words, we rob them of our concern, our care, and our interest in their well-being. This is a tough topic, with all kinds of hardships at stake, but our faith would have us navigating through storms, not running from them. Our mandate is to be a people of reconciliation!

In The Pages

What opportunities do you have this Christmas to make some things right with your family? When was the last time you showed your parents or in-laws your appreciation? Can you find something to say or do that will edify them? Don't you think it's time to lay down those old offenses?

Order Already!

December 20
Proverbs 20

"Counsel in the heart of man is like deep water; but a man of understanding will draw it out." Proverbs 20:5, KJV

Have you ever been in a restaurant with someone who absolutely cannot decide what to order off the menu? Every single option has to be carefully considered! This usually leads to the waiter having to explain how the food is prepared, where it was caught, and what it is served with. Another grueling 10 minutes will then be required to make this oh-so-important decision. Maybe that's the equivalent of culinary foreplay, who knows?

I'll just have my cheeseburger-cooked medium, with jalapenos, please. Boom! Done! I've usually decided before we even find our table. Maybe it's just me.

We do get stuck.

Today's verse is encouraging us to put action to whatever that thing is deep inside of us. We can't be content to just think about doing something, to plan a change, or to contemplate a move. At some point, we have to do something about it.

Wisdom says we should *draw it out*. We ought to grab that *"it"* and do something with *"it."* *"It"* could be anything! But going after *"it,"* whatever *"it"* is, will invoke faith and courage. We might fall in the process, but we'll at least fall forward and pull ourselves into something new!

In 2 Timothy 3, the Apostle Paul offers some disturbing insight as to what some of the dysfunction will look like as we move closer to the end of time. There is almost always a pointless debate raging somewhere about that stuff, so I'm not going to get into any of that here.

Anyway, Paul prophesied an interesting thought about people being prone to indecisiveness. Some people just will not make a decision until they are absolutely forced to:

"always learning and never able to come to the knowledge of the truth"
(2 Timothy 3:7, NASB).

The Greek word for *"knowledge"* is **ĕpignōsis** (pronounced *ep-ig´-no-sis*), which is a *"discernment"* or *"recognition"* knowing. I love this!

Everything in me screams,

WE ARE THE WILL OF GOD! TRUST YOUR HEART!

TRUST GOD'S VOICE!

DRAW OUT THE TRUTH and LETS GET ON WITH IT!

DECIDE ALREADY AND GO FOR IT!

Christians today live with too much fear and rejection! God will tell us NO if He has to. He can also redeem a mistake. So what are we so afraid of?

Draw deep, pull out the deeper waters, and put it out there for the world to see! We are all waiting!

In The Pages

Is there a word of change inside of you that is waiting for you to do something with it? How long have you known that word was down in there? What are you waiting on? You could be delaying a great blessing, reward, or journey. Quit stalling.

Funky On The Inside

December 21
Proverbs 21

"Every way of a man is right in his own eyes, but the Lord weighs the hearts. To do righteousness and justice is more acceptable to the Lord than sacrifice." Proverbs 21:2-3, NKJV

I wanted to present these two verses together today because we need to be reminded regularly that the Lord cares much more about our hearts than what we do ceremonially. There's nothing wrong with ceremonies and rituals if our hearts are right. But God does not prefer ceremony over heart. It's just that simple. We forget that.

We get to thinking God applauds our outward works. Whatever we do in the name of God (worship, giving, serving, etc.), our heart is what matters to Him, not the actual deed.

Because we live under a new covenant, the days of sacrificial rituals are dead and gone. We are under a far better system. But too often, we drag up the old stuff and think God gets chill bumps because of some ritual.

Jesus rarely got hot under the collar, but it was this kind of stuff that set Him off. Middle easterners are already passionate by nature, but I imagine spit was flying when Jesus got worked up over the antics of the religious professionals.

"Woe to you, scribes and Pharisees, hypocrites! For you tithe mint and dill and cummin, and have neglected the weightier provisions of the law: **justice and mercy and faithfulness***; but these are the things you should have done without neglecting the others. You blind guides, who strain out a gnat and swallow a camel! Woe to you, scribes and Pharisees, hypocrites! For you clean the outside of the cup and of the dish, but inside they are full of robbery and self-indulgence. You blind Pharisee, first clean the inside of the cup and of the dish, so that the outside of it may become clean also. Woe to you, scribes and Pharisees, hypocrites! For you are like whitewashed tombs, which on the outside appear beautiful, but inside they are full of dead men's bones and all uncleanness. So you, too, outwardly appear righteous to men, but inwardly you are full of hypocrisy and lawlessness"* (Matthew 23:23-28, NASB).

The Gospels are absolutely full of incidents of Jesus confronting religious devils and exposing religious facades. My concern is that we don't recognize our own pharisaical tendencies.

To think that Jesus' only issue was with the Jews' religious bureaucracy would be to miss the point entirely!

The scribes and Pharisees were causing roadblocks for John and Jane Doe to "get to" the Lord. But remember, God cares more about our heart than our works.

"Faith without works is dead" (James 2:20, KJV) is true enough, but if real faith is involved, our hearts are always being tested in the process. Let's move away from our concerns about image, style, and personal preference in worship and service.

He wants to get to the heart of the matter: your heart—my heart.

In The Pages

Would you do the stuff you do for God if no one else was watching? Would you do the stuff you do for the Lord if no one recognized you for it? Are you sure about that?

Mother Mocker

December 22
Proverbs 22

"Drive out the mocker, and out goes strife; quarrels and insults are ended." Proverbs 22:10, NIV

"Now Sarah saw the son of Hagar the Egyptian, whom she had borne to Abraham, mocking. Therefore she said to Abraham, 'Drive out this maid and her son, for the son of this maid shall not be an heir with my son Isaac.'" Genesis 21:9-10, NASB

It seemed like the perfect plan . . . until the promise showed up.

Sarah and Hagar were in agreement. Abraham was happy to help out however a brother could, even to the point of spilling his ancient seed. Then Hagar conceives. And like a child who doesn't have enough money to go to the circus, Sarah has to watch from a distance for the next nine months as Abraham rubs and blesses Hagar's belly.

When it came time to deliver, Sarah slid underneath Hagar in support, but also perhaps to signify herself as Ishmael's birth mommy. But in the end, the child belonged to Abraham and Hagar.

Sarah was on the outside looking in.

How long would this arrangement work? Two mommies under one roof? Sarah was pretending, and she would never feel fulfilled this way. Something had to give.

"God is not a man, that He should lie" (Numbers 23:19, KJV).

Sarah becomes pregnant with Isaac, the child of promise, the faith child, the miracle, the unthinkable, unexplainable, the child of the Spirit! Sarah's mourning turns to dancing! Things are finally in order.

Oh . . . wait. Things are not in order! Now we have one father in the house (church), but two very different women with two very different children. Ishmael was born of a slave, conceived by works. Isaac was born of the freewoman, the woman of covenant—via a conception orchestrated by the Holy Spirit.

Paul wrote to the church in Galatia, using this very story as a reminder of Who it is that determines the agenda and direction for the body of Christ:

"And you brethren, like Isaac, are children of promise. But as at that time he who was born according to the flesh persecuted him who was born according to the Spirit, so it is now also. But what does the Scripture say? Cast out the bondwoman and her son, for the son of the bondwoman shall not be an heir with the son of the free woman. So then, brethren, we are not children of a bondwoman, but of the free woman" (Galatians 4:28-31, NASB).

We are no longer under the old dead law.

Paul challenges us to stop running the church based on carnal perspectives and man's preferences. The call is to sow to the Spirit. The call is to move towards faith and dependency on God, not the dead rituals and good works of the past.

In Galatians 5 we are reminded, *"If we live by the Spirit, let us also walk by the Spirit."* (V:25, NASB). The church today, much like Abraham and Sarah's home, still finds itself conflicted over who calls the shots.

Works of the flesh, versus sowing to the Holy Spirit and living by faith... which one? These things are diametrically opposed and cannot coexist. Today's wisdom declares that the mommy and child of *works only* have got to go!

In The Pages

Which child is the leader in your church, Ishmael or Isaac? How do you know? Are the people in your church led by faith?

Tightwads

December 23
Proverbs 23

"Don't accept a meal from a tightwad; don't expect anything special. He'll be as stingy with you as he is with himself; he'll say, "Eat! Drink!" but won't mean a word of it. His miserly serving will turn your stomach when you realize the meal's a sham." Proverbs 23:6-8, MSG

The Hebrew describes this person as someone with an evil eye (*a stingy miser, consumed with selfishness*). Peterson uses the word "*tightwad,*" which is perfect for the concept. Wisdom says to beware of accepting gifts from someone we know to be selfish with an unhealthy habit of penny-pinching excessiveness.

What happens is that you make the mistake of offending this person; overstepping some imaginary boundary he or she has set. Liberty and freedom scares the hell out of these people! Without warning, you'll begin to sense that the air has changed. There are all kinds of issues with accepting favors from or trying to accomplish much of anything with a cheapskate.

Even in the old law, there were specific instructions about not being money-grubbing misers (Deuteronomy 15:6-11). Heck, if people living under the old dead law could be generous with their stuff and recognize how blessed they were, how much more should we, who live under the freedom of a new and expansive covenant, be generous with our stuff?

We bless because we have been blessed!

Ike, one of my dearest friends, has the body and strength of a bull and the heart of a tender child. He will do just about anything for anyone at anytime. Being a full-time fireman allows him a lot of room for odd jobs and service projects for the elderly.

Folklore has it that one spring, Ike needed to borrow a rotor-tiller from a deacon in the church for a garden project. The deacon was extremely gracious and granted Ike's request to borrow his barely-used tiller. When Ike arrived to load the tiller into the back of his brand new pickup truck, the deacon gave him all the operating instructions. The tiller was too heavy for even Ike to physically pick up, so he decided to lean a couple of boards onto the back tailgate and just walk the running tiller up into the bed of the truck.

With the tiller roaring to a pretty high rpm, it crawled right up those boards in a hurry as Ike screamed, *"Where's the kill switch?"* Too late!

The tiller kept right on climbing, up the back of the cab, onto the roof, down the windshield, onto the hood (chewing and clawing everything in its path), and eventually fell to the ground and spun in a stationary circle on its side.

Now, a stingy man would have probably hired assassins to take out my buddy. Instead, there was laughter and gratitude that no one got hurt. Graceful laughter is good medicine!

Just monitor and take note of whom you are dealing with. Stuff happens, and a miser is always keeping score! Free ain't always free.

In The Pages

Do you pride yourself in frugality? How easy can you give away your stuff? What do you think is behind a hoarding spirit? Ever had dealings with a tightwad? Describe how it left you feeling.

Believe

Christmas Eve

"And this will be the sign to you: You will find a Babe wrapped in swaddling cloths, lying in a manger." Luke 2:12, NKJV

Not long ago, I stopped by the local BBQ joint for a takeout lunch. A woman was waiting for her order while her four-year-old daughter sat next to her, putting the finishing touches on her letter to Santa. This kid was absolutely beautiful! Mocha skin, green eyes, beautiful hair!

So I started asking her about her list. It was little girl stuff mostly, nothing big. Then I asked her how she thought she was going to get what she was asking for? When she looked up at me, her face looked like an angel. Her eyes were absolutely on fire! It took my breath away really.

She said, "Santa is coming see me!" Well, of course that was the answer I had expected to get. But the fire in her eyes was this pure and innocent **"faith"** that had the essence of His mustard seed that can move a mountain. In that moment, it felt holy to me that she genuinely "believed" in anything!

She could have said Donald Duck and it would have had the same effect on me. Time will take care of the Santa thing for her, but the fact that she *believes* is what our wind-chapped world so desperately needs.

Are we willing to believe and trust that God will orchestrate for our good?

A simple spark of faith and a risking belief (actually doing stuff) can put us in a position to receive real Kingdom life. The earth groans for these dynamics to manifest with His people!

The Godhead determined that He, *"a Babe,"* would come solely for a sacrificial purpose.

JESUS WHOLLY DEMONSTRATED THAT HIS LIFE WAS NOT ABOUT HIMSELF!

The Apostle Paul said it perfectly:

"Have this attitude in yourselves which was also in Christ Jesus, who, although He existed in the form of God, did not regard equality with God a thing to be grasped, but emptied Himself, taking the form of a bond-servant, and being made in the likeness of men. Being found in appearance as a man, He humbled Himself by becoming obedient to the point of death, even death on a cross. For this reason also, God highly exalted Him, and bestowed on Him the name which is above every name, so that at the name of Jesus EVERY KNEE WILL BOW, of those who are in heaven and on earth and under the earth, and that every tongue will confess that Jesus Christ is Lord, to the glory of God the Father!" (Philippians 2:5-11, NASB)

He made His own life about you and me. How much better would our own lives be if we could live in that kind of Kingdom mindset? **It is NOT about me!**

It's not easy to get there, especially when most everyone around us isn't geared up to go that route. Can we really believe for such a thing?

Are we willing to believe we actually get life back by giving away ours, by showing love, mercy, forgiveness, and risky faith?

What a Gift we have been given! What a Gift we have to release! It's a perfect day to lay it all out there!

MERRY CHRISTMAS!

In The Pages

Who would benefit most from your attention today? Who would be the most surprised by your genuine care and concern? What would "risky faith" look like on a day like today?

Prince

Christmas

"For a child will be born to us, a son will be given to us; and the government will rest on His shoulders; and His name will be called Wonderful Counselor, Mighty God, Eternal Father, Prince of Peace. There will be no end to the increase of His government or of peace, on the throne of David and over his kingdom, to establish it and to uphold it with justice and righteousness from then on and forevermore. The zeal of the Lord of hosts will accomplish this." Isaiah 9:6-7, NASB

Perhaps the most beautiful prophetic declaration ever! Such words are most assuredly beyond our comprehension and appreciation. *"A CHILD will be BORN to US, a SON will be GIVEN to US."*

It is the most magnificent wonder ever!

I want us to ponder one of this child's many names: *"Prince of Peace."* Obviously, the Hebrew prophecy points to the Messiah as the head, governor, or captain of all peace. But to get the full impact, you need to see the word *Prince* used in terms of its New Testament designation (Acts 3:15, 5:31).

Again, the word *Prince*, or **archēgŏs** (pronounced *ar-khay-gos'*), means *"captain, chief leader, or highest ruler."* What few realize is that the **archēgŏs** was also the description of a very important job on ships that sailed the beautiful waters of the Mediterranean.

There were all sorts of complications in trying to dock a ship in those dicey waters. Small hidden reefs are common in the Med., so instead of trying to land in the shallows near a shoreline, the ships would drop anchor in deep water.

Then, the **archēgŏs** would tie a rope around his waist and swim through the treacherous waters, over the dangerous reefs, and onto shore, where he would fasten the rope to a tree (or whatever else) to offer a secure line from ship to shore. Then a smaller dinghy could use the secured rope to safely maneuver passengers, supplies, and other cargo to shore.

"But now Christ has been raised from the dead, the first fruits of those who are asleep. For since by a man came death, by a man also came the resurrection of the dead. For as in Adam all die, so also in Christ all will be made alive. But each in his own order: Christ the first fruits, after that those who are Christ's at His coming, then comes the end, when He hands over the kingdom to the God and Father, when He has abolished all rule and all authority and power. For He must reign until He has put all His enemies under His feet. The last enemy that will be abolished is death" (1 Corinthians 15:20-26, NASB).

Our **Archēgŏs**, our Captain, our First Fruits, our Prince, the one and only Jesus Christ, swam through those hostile waters of death and secured the way for you and me to cross over into eternal life! Death does not have the final say.

LIFE awaits us on the other side! It's all done! That *child* came with our safe passage in mind!

May His conquering spirit and overcoming love bless and enrich your heart as we celebrate the coming of our Prince! Merry Christmas, everyone! Merry Christmas! Mike & Patti xo

Dead Legs

December 26
Proverbs 26

"Like a lame man's legs that hang limp is a proverb in the mouth of a fool."
Proverbs 26:7, NIV

Martin Luther had a poignant rendering of this verse: *"Like dancing to a cripple, so is a proverb in the mouth of a fool."*[17] We don't use the word "cripple" too much anymore. The way we refer to people with disabilities can be a touchy subject. Whatever word we use, we get the picture.

I see a strong young man or woman, looking down at atrophied muscles and twisted limbs that are supposed to be strong and mobile, laying dormant on the footrest of a wheelchair. It must be the most frustrating thing! Of course, these challenges do not reflect upon character and mental capacities. To assume such would be a gross miscalculation.

Solomon's point is that lack of character and insight is the thing that actually cripples the fool. A fool can quote proverbs and intelligent concepts all day long, but if his character and maturity is underdeveloped—all will disregard him. He is his own worst enemy.

A fool portrays himself as strong, but is not strong at all. A fool may sound impressive at first, but there is nothing impressive about him. A fool will sound mature, but consistently reveals self-seeking immaturity. He has all the tools of wisdom at his disposal, but not a clue how to use any of them.

I can't help but think how we could easily substitute the word "religion" for the word *"proverb"* in today's focus text.

Consider these words by the Apostle Paul:

"I was with you in weakness and in fear and in much trembling, and my message and my preaching were not in persuasive words of wisdom, but in demonstration of the Spirit and of power, so that your faith would not rest on the wisdom of men, but on the power of God" (1 Corinthians 2:3-5, NASB).

If our relationship with God is based on *persuasive words* and intellectual concept, lacking heart, passion, and commitment, then we are like the cripple bound to his wheelchair. It may look good on the outside, but it's ultimately lame and powerless.

Our relationship with God has to be centered on the *demonstration of the Spirit and His power*! Religion is a lame attempt to please God in our own efforts. Some of what we do and what we say has nothing to do with God's desire for us at all.

Much like the fool with his Proverbs, we quote scriptures and put up a good front, but we don't allow the things we say to really change us or affect the way we live. We have to break out of this ideal that following God is a "church or ministry" activity.

What flows from our hearts is what really matters. That is the internal substance God acts on.

In The Pages

Have you ever wondered if you might be religiously crippled? Are you willing to ask for honest feedback about your religious habits? How much of your time do you give to *"pure religion"* (James 1:27)?

Useless Expenditure

December 27
Proverbs 27

"Carrying a log across your shoulders while you're hefting a boulder with your arms is nothing compared to the burden of putting up with a fool." Proverbs 27:3, MSG

"A stone is heavy and the sand weighty, but the provocation of a fool is heavier than both of them." Proverbs 27:3, NASB

It's simple. *"Putting up with a fool"* is as draining to you mentally and emotionally as hauling brick and timber is to you physically. The Hebrew uses the word **kaʻas** (pronounced *kahʹ-as*), which translates as *"provocation, anger, grief, indignation, spite, sorrow*, and *wrath."* Obviously, this stuff isn't pretty!

This same word is used in 1 Samuel 1:16, when Hannah told Eli how *provoked* she felt. Everything seemed to be against her. She was sharing her husband with her tormentor, her womb was closed, and even though Elkanah loved her, he couldn't identify with her pain! She was worn out over the whole ordeal! I can't begin to imagine how grief-stricken and aggravated she must have been with her situation!

Women under these kinds of pressures tend to make national headlines:

"Man's body parts recovered in 15 different states."
(Ewwww.... lovely)

I wonder if Jesus was referring to any of this when He said, *"...but whoever causes one of these little ones who believe in Me to stumble, it would be better for him to have a heavy millstone hung around his neck, and to be drowned in the depth of the sea"* (Matthew 18:6, NASB).

The context was about rank, self-honor, religious positioning, and stumbling blocks. The "God business" had gotten so out of control with so many misconceptions about what was important to God, they had forgotten about simple acts of love. The notion that a child could be valued and loved by the Lord because they simply existed was unheard of to these people!

Almost everything out there was ridiculously misconstrued. Jesus had to be exhausted from dealing with such mindsets!

It was a horrible way for His life to end here on earth. I wonder if Jesus' fatigue in confronting so many religious fools made his transition any easier at all? In the garden, his sweat was as great drops of blood. His prayer was in agony. The fatigue and the burden of the trail he had walked and the path he was about to take had to be overwhelming! Considering all this, it should motivate us to spend less time in dialogue with religious devils and use more time serving those willing to hear and receive freedom.

Forget about the people who just want to argue and debate.

There are people out there, wounded, hungry, sick, and hurting, who are willing to hear you out. They're always surprised when we reach out to them. But we need this truth just as much as they do, if not more! We need to be refreshed!

Trying to convince religious fools of anything is a waste of time and precious energy.

In The Pages

How deep are the religious waters you swim in? Are you trying to get out, or just treading water? How easily do people perceive that you are full of His love?

What A Frikk'n Waste!

December 28
Proverbs 28

"Because of the transgression of a land, many are its princes; but by a man of understanding and knowledge, right will be prolonged." Proverbs 28:2, NKJV

You can get a whole belly full of what this verse is talking about by reading 1 Kings 16:8-13 and 2 Kings 15:8-15. Israel was to be governed by theocratic principles, which put more pressure on the leaders to seek God's ways and counsel. When the leaders chose not to live by God's ways, *transgression* in the land resulted in frequent turnover at the top and unleashed civil unrest and chaos.

"Transgression" is the NASB translation for **pesha'** (pronounced *peh'-shah*), which means *"national (moral or religious) rebellion or sin."*

Corrupt action by leaders equates to social, spiritual, and political unrest.

When King Saul refused to govern by proper protocol, the prophet Samuel said to him,

"For rebellion is as the sin of witchcraft, and stubbornness is as iniquity and idolatry. Because you have rejected the word of the Lord, He also has rejected you from being king" (1 Samuel 15:23, NKJV).

Absolutely haunting! God has a very low tolerance for witchcraft and spiritual usurpation!

The story of Absalom's rebellion (2 Samuel 13-20) is one of those heart-wrenching episodes in scripture that leaves us shaking our heads and mouthing the words,

"Arrrgggg! What a frikk'n waste!"

To say that David did not handle things properly with Absalom would be a gross understatement! It seems David's parenting skills were lacking at times.

Absalom had endured quite a bit of mistreatment from his father. His rebellion was almost understandable, but that doesn't make it just. He allowed anger and bitterness to eat away at him until they eventually led him to his own death.

When a child is controlled, abused, or totally ignored, it leads to rejection issues and eventually rebellion. Kids don't just decide to rebel against their parents. That's not how God created us. Something goes wrong along the way that causes a child to turn from his parents' love.

Maybe there are secrets inside the home. Maybe the heavy hand of religion and control leaves the kid desperate for a little bit of freedom.

When you shake a champagne bottle too many times, it's eventually going to pop!

As ugly as this story turned out—as unjust as it was—Absalom is responsible for the decisions he made. His father had once lived in exile from someone he loved and never once lifted his hand to strike back at his authority.

Absalom's rebellion cost him his life. Such a waste!

In The Pages

What do you think it means to be "rebellious"? What could Absalom have done differently? I've heard it said, *"The true test of our ability to honor is when we follow bad leaders."* What are your thoughts on that?

Wildfire

December 29
Proverbs 29

"Scorners set a city aflame, but wise men turn away anger." Proverbs 29:8, NASB

"Now it came about after this that Absalom provided for himself a chariot and horses and fifty men as runners before him. Absalom used to rise early and stand beside the way to the gate; and when any man had a suit to come to the king for judgment, Absalom would call to him and say, 'From what city are you?' And he would say, 'Your servant is from one of the tribes of Israel.' Then Absalom would say to him, 'See, your claims are good and right, but no man

listens to you on the part of the king.' Moreover, Absalom would say, 'Oh that one would appoint me judge in the land, then every man who has any suit or cause could come to me and I would give him justice.' And when a man came near to prostrate himself before him, he would put out his hand and take hold of him and kiss him. In this manner Absalom dealt with all Israel who came to the king for judgment; so Absalom stole away the hearts of the men of Israel."
2 Samuel 15:1-6, NASB

A *scorn*-full man is an arrogant man, a presumptuous mocker. The Prince made a drastic move in Chapter 14 when he burned Joab's field in order to coerce him into going to the king on his behalf. At first, it appeared that father and son had buried the hatchet and put things back in proper order. Obviously Absalom's heart was not genuine when he prostrated himself before the King. Absalom had burned before. He was about to burn again.

The word for *"aflame"* is **pûwach** (pronounced *poo'-akh*). It means, *"to breathe, blow, or puff upon a situation only to kindle fire, scorn or discontent."* The arrogant mocker (Absalom), full of unresolved bitterness, begins to blow upon the minds of the people of Israel, intercepting them before they can get to King David.

What starts out as emotional undermining, evolves into a full-blown insurrection! The city, "the people"—all buys into Absalom's rebellion.

"So Absalom stole away the hearts..." (2 Samuel 15:6, NASB)

There it is: insubordination in its purest form!

The good thing about spiritual government is that it's always engaged.

The bad thing about spiritual government is that it's always engaged.

The smallest adjustment to proper protocol can bring such destruction upon ourselves, and those around us. Grasping for power, maneuvering for control, planting seeds of discontent via gossip, and other undermining tactics will only unleash a firestorm that can't be maintained.

Wisdom clearly says we need to deal with our anger and disappointment. We have more than enough opportunities to purge the poisons. His blood can and will cleanse our minds and heal our hearts. Let it!

In The Pages

Read Isaiah 53 again. List some of the offenses the Messiah suffered. How did He respond to such injustices? We benefited from his suffering. How is this possible?

Keepin' It Real

December 30
Proverbs 30

"Two things I request of You (deprive me not before I die): Remove falsehood and lies far from me; give me neither poverty nor riches—feed me with the food allotted to me; lest I be full and deny You, and say, "Who is the Lord?" or lest I be poor and steal, and profane the name of my God." Proverbs 30:7-9, NKJV

It's hard to believe we are wrapping up another year, isn't it? We're in that doorway, about to step out of this year and into the next. I appreciate the heart of Agur in this prayer. He comes to the Lord with his dying requests. I believe his requests are based on practical past experiences, rather than prophetic foresight.

Much like the character Jean Valjean in Hugo's *Les Misérables*, he has lived in the pain of differing opportunities. He won some; he lost some. I think we can all identify with that.

When I look back over some of the things that happened this year, I think, *Geez Paschall, you blew that!* But I can also look back and see where grace showed up and where I got much better than I deserved or my actions warranted.

I like the man's request—it helps me reflect back, as I look forward.

Some believe that Agur was Solomon. There is no factual proof, though the humility of the request seems to align with Solomon's heart. It just feels weird that a man who has always been coated in royalty would request such moderation.

I suspect that Solomon's (if it is indeed Solomon) initial request for wisdom actually manifested in a true ability to prophetically identify with the subjects he ruled and those of us who still glean from his writings. Think about what the writer requested: **PROTECTION** (from falsehood) and **PROVISION** (not too much, not too little).

You can pretty much summarize all of our fears around those two things: **PROTECTION** and **PROVISION!** You might have so much trouble with the whole "faith" concept of God's goodness and His desire for us to have everything we want that you can't see this. But the fact that we've pursued God so vehemently about these two things validates how much fear we actually have around those concerns.

Agur was very in touch with his humanness. Here is an example: *"I am too stupid to be human, and I lack common sense. I have not mastered human wisdom, nor do I know the Holy One."* (Proverbs 30:2-3, NLT). I give the man a lot of credit for asking for divine help with these issues!

Ultimately, Agur did not want to dishonor God's reputation. He wanted his actions to validate the impressions God had made on his heart. He wanted to live in integrity with his life as an open book. He wanted anyone who witnessed how he handled the circumstances of his life to easily recognize the influence of a loving, good, and gracious God.

There is a great passage in Deuteronomy 8:1-17 that challenges the people of the wilderness to consider all that He had done for them during their 40 years of wandering. He warned them of pride and encouraged them to be grateful and considerate.

He called them into a confident moderation that said, ***"Thank You Lord!"*** Counsel well taken!

In The Pages

So how was this last year? Do you see where God provided? Do you see where He protected? Can you see any good? How does it help you prepare to transition into next year?

New Year Revolution

December 31

"...knowing this, that our old self was crucified with Him, in order that our body of sin might be done away with, so that we would no longer be slaves to sin; for he who has died is freed from sin." Romans 6:6-7, NASB

One of my best friends tells a story that demonstrates the powerful truth of this passage. Growing up in the tough streets of Pontiac, MI, Michael had plenty of opportunities to see humanity at its weakest.

Although there was more than enough conflict in his own home, Michael's father frequently had to bear arms and intervene at the neighbor's house when Mr. Taylor would drink too much. Jack Taylor was a mean drunk, a fighting drunk, which put Mrs. Taylor and the kids in harm's way on a fairly regular basis.

Many years after moving away, Michael returned to his old stomping grounds and paid a visit to the Taylor home. Mrs. Taylor was plenty cordial and extremely welcoming. Michael asked her, *"How's Jack? Has he stopped drinking?"* Her response said it all: *"Jack is dead. He doesn't get drunk anymore!"*

It's a simple truth.

WE DO NOT HAVE TO LIVE IN SIN!

We can come into agreement with the completed work of the cross that defeated the power of sin and death over our lives! We can actually say no the things that once controlled and manipulated us. We no longer have to be slaves. We have a choice! We have been crucified with Him!

I once heard my friend Anthony Chapman teach a principle I had never really considered before.[18] Traditionally, we use this day to make New Year Resolutions for some positive change in our lives. We're going to exercise more and lose weight, or learn a new skill, or quit smoking, maybe even repair some relationships. But we do it every year—don't we?

What motivates us to actually follow through with our resolution is that we change our minds or restructure our thoughts. The problem is that we too easily lose that motivation by the end of January! Too many great intentions are discarded like a soiled paper napkin.

I know that a couple of days after New Years, the health club where I work out will be full of enthused new members in their cute little workout clothes and dazzling new running shoes. By February 75 percent of them will be done and dusted (though still probably paying their dues).

We like the idea of a positive change, but are we willing to do the real work?

Instead of a New Year's resolution, Chapman says we need a New Year's *Revolution*! That means something old has to die, so something new can be born. The old regime, the old thing that has power in your life now, has to die. Then, the Spirit will birth this new thing in you, with new power!

You need a Jack Taylor! Yes, you need to change your mind, but you also need to activate the truth that God will help you overcome—in the Spirit and in the natural!

So before you make some resolution of how you're going to change, why not first identify what needs to die? Then, call upon the power of Christ to transform your thoughts and actions.

Prophesy and activate your spirit to come into alignment with that power to change. Then expect to move toward that thing or change what needs to happen next year with the full expectation of complete victory!

In The Pages

First things first, what needs to die so something else can live?

ENDNOTES

October 4 – [1]Prophet Bob Jones. Don't ask me to explain this. Bob sees and says a bunch of things I can't explain. No reflection on Bob... just me.

October 13 - [2]I wrote that quote from Richard Rohr in my journal from one of his books or publications. I can't remember where I found it nor can I find the quote. I contacted Father Richard and he doesn't remember the source either. Guess you'll just have take my word for it.

October 15 – [3]Peter Mutebi. I've lost touch with Peter. Such a sweet man.

October 24 – [4]Just a little shout out for my son by marriage. Jon Egan is the leader of Desperation Band and lead Pastor of Worship at New Life Church in Colorado Springs, CO. A ridiculous talent and evidently he has good taste and sense... (he married my daughter Paige in 2003). They have three children: Isabel Rose, Jones Michael, and Lewis Christian. http://desperationband.com

October 25 – [5]Ira and Judy Milligan have been doing ministry a long time. Ira is a close friend, a skilled counselor, seasoned Prophet, and an excellent teacher of God's word! http://servant-ministries.org

October 29 – [6]I want to recommend a little book to you. It's a very short read, but extremely insightful and powerful! *If I Perish, I Perish* by Major W. Ian Thomas. One of my favorites on Esther!

November 4 – [7]Here is a link to videos that tell the story: www.daystar.com/ondemand/video/?video=5062160203001

November 6 – [8]Seth Godin - www.sethgodin.com, November 5, 2010. Used by permission.

November 10 – [9]Not all High School football coaches are douche bags. Yes, I have forgiven him. But this guy had personal issues. The overwhelming majority of coaches really love and serve the kids well.

November 11 – [10]Rev. D. Michael Toby (Feb. 18, 1947 - Dec. 29, 2012). Mike was the guy that first made me believe that I belonged in full-time ministry. We were almost inseparable from 1982-1991. He was a true discipler and a real mentor. By his example, I learned how to preach, lead, and love the Church. I loved him dearly. Mike was Sr. Pastor of FBC-Woodway, in Waco, Tx for 35 years. He is survived by his beautiful wife Jackie, two sons: Josh married to Olya, and Scott married to Monica, and 4 grandchildren: Evan, Conrad, Marlena, and Gisele.

November 12 – [11]Don and Christine Potter are some amazing people. Don is a master musician and an authentic spiritual psalmist. If you've never listened to his worship CD's... get on it! Without a doubt, he is one the most anointed worship guys I've ever been around.

November 18 – [12]You can get more ideas from this discussion in Richard Rohr's *From Wild Man to Wise Man: Reflections on Male Spirituality*. St. Anthony Messenger Press.

November 22 – [13]The book I purchased and read was *Lovis Corinth: California Studies in the History of Art (Book 27)*, by Horst Uhr. Published in 1990 by University of California Press, 1st edition.

November 26 - [14]Michael R. Hindes sermon notes. Used by permission.

December 1 – [15]Richard Rohr O.F.M. Prayer taken from his sermon tape series *Preparing for Christmas: Daily Meditations for Advent*, published by Franciscan Media. Used by permission.

December 4 - [16]About the time I turned 48, I discovered *Adam's Return: The Five Promises of Male Initiation*. That book summarized what I had felt and known for a long time, but couldn't put words to it. The stuff Father Richard taught in that book really rocked me. I still believe what he teaches is true.

December 26 – [17]Jamieson, R., Fausset, A. R., & Brown, D. (1871). *Commentary Critical and Explanatory on the Whole Bible*. (Public Domain).

December 31 – [18]Anthony Chapman is the lead Teaching Pastor at The Rock of York Church, York, England. He's a brilliant communicator and excellent teacher of God's Word. But... don't expect normal. He's anything but normal. www.rockchurch.org.uk

RESOURCES

BIBLE KEY:

KJV - *The Holy Bible, King James Version* (Public Domain).

MSG – Peterson, E. H. (2005). *The Message: the Bible in contemporary language*. Colorado Springs, CO: NavPress. Used by permission.

NASB - *New American Standard Bible: 1995 update*. (1995). LaHabra, CA: The Lockman Foundation. Used by permission.

LXX - Brenton, L. C. L. (1870). *The Septuagint Version of the Old Testament: English Translation*. London: Samuel Bagster and Sons.

NCV - *The Everyday Bible: New Century Version*. (2005). Nashville, TN: Thomas Nelson, Inc. Used by permission.

NET - Biblical Studies Press. (2006). *The NET Bible First Edition; Bible. English. NET Bible.; The NET Bible*. Biblical Studies Press. Used by permission.

NIV – *THE HOLY BIBLE, NEW INTERNATIONAL VERSION®*. Copyright © 1973, 1978, 1984 by International Bible Society. Used by permission.

NKJV - *The New King James Version*. (1982). Nashville: Thomas Nelson. Used by permission.

NLT - *New Living Translation* (1996, 2005, 2007). Tyndale House Publishers, Inc., Carol Stream, Illinois 60188. Used by permission.

NRSV - *The Holy Bible: New Revised Standard Version*. (1989). Nashville: Thomas Nelson Publishers. Used by permission.

RSV - *Revised Standard Version of the Bible*, copyright 1952 [2nd edition, 1971] by the Division of Christian Education of the National Council of the Churches of Christ in the United States of America. Used by permission.

TLB – *The Living Bible* (1971) Tyndale House Publishers, Inc., Wheaton, IL 60189. Used by permission.

YLT - *The Young's Literal Translation Bible* (Public Domain).

OTHER HELPS:

Baxter, J. Sidlow (1960). *Awake My Heart*. Copyright © 1960. Zondervan Publishing Company, Grand Rapids, MI.

Blue, J. R. (1985). James. (J. F. Walvoord & R. B. Zuck, Eds.)*The Bible Knowledge Commentary: An Exposition of the Scriptures*. Wheaton, IL: Victor Books.

Chambers, Oswald (1935). Original edition © 1935. *My Utmost For His Highest*. Dodd, Mead & Company, Inc., New York, NY.

Jamieson, R., Fausset, A. R., & Brown, D. (1871). *Commentary Critical and Explanatory on the Whole Bible*. (Public Domain).

Keil, C. F., & Delitzsch, F. (1996). *Commentary on the Old Testament*. Peabody, MA: Hendrickson.

Peterson, Eugene H. (2007). *Conversations: THE MESSAGE with It's Translator*. Copyright © 2007 by Eugene H. Peterson. All rights reserved. THE MESSAGE Numbered Edition copyright © 2005. NavPress Publishing Group, Colorado Springs, CO.

Rohr, Richard. *Adam's Return: The Five Promises of Male Initiation*. Copyright © 2004. Crossroad Publishing Company, New York, NY. Used with permission.

Rohr, Richard. Preparing for Christmas: Daily Meditations for Advent. Copyright © 2008. Franciscan Media, Cincinnati, OH. Used with permission.

Rohr, Richard and Feister, John. *Radical Grace: Daily Meditations by Richard Rohr*. Copyright © 1995. St. Anthony Messengers Press, Cincinnati, OH. Used with permission.

Ryrie, Charles Caldwell (1995). *The Ryrie Study Bible, New American Standard*: with introductions, annotations, outlines, marginal references, harmony of the Gospels, synopsis of Bible doctrine, index of Scripture, index to notes, concordance, maps, and timeline charts, and many other helps. Expanded edition. Scripture taken from the NEW AMERICAN STANDARD BIBLE®, Copyright© 1960, 1962, 1963, 1968, 1971, 1972, 1973, 1975, 1994 by the Lockman Foundation. Used by permission.

Strong, J. (2009). *A Concise Dictionary of the Words in the Greek Testament and The Hebrew Bible*. Bellingham, WA: Logos Bible Software.

Thomas, R. L. (1998). *New American Standard Hebrew-Aramaic and Greek dictionaries : updated edition*. Anaheim: Foundation Publications, Inc.

Thomas, R. L., The Lockman Foundation. (1998). *New American Standard exhaustive concordance of the Bible: updated edition*. Anaheim: Foundation Publications, Inc.

ACKNOWLDEGEMENTS

I would be remiss if I didn't thank some people. Patti Paschall, the love of my life, is the one who prodded me the most to start putting my thoughts on paper. For over 35 years, she's been the one to lead the charge to encourage me. No one has believed in me more. Her "I love this" has been quite the life source. She is my Jesus with skin. She has everything to do with my finishing this project. I can't imagine such a venture without her being beside me. My one, my only, my queen. xo

My children and grandchildren also provide the most amazing motivation to spill the goods. My girls and their guys are spiritually very serious and engaged. They're on the edge, and they push me to peak over their ledge from time to time. I love their views. Nicole, Steve, Paige, and Jon: I could not be more blessed by you. xo

One thought that really helped me chill out and be real was the idea that one day my grandbabies will be Kingdom fire-breathers. They'll be much more aggressive in the Spirit than myself, but maybe there is enough here to feed them for a season or two. Isabel Rose, Jones Michael, Lewis Christian, Grace Irene, and those to follow: you are perfection in my heart! xo

I wrote and compiled the first month of devos in January 2010 and presented them to 18 of my intimate peers. I asked them for honest feedback. A few did indeed respond, but the majority never said a word. To those few who did respond, I got some major encouragement. Thank you.

In fact, it was my son-in-law, Jon, who drove the decisive nail when he asked me, *"Ba, who is your audience?"* Baaamm! I knew this project wasn't necessarily going to be for "church people." Anyone was welcome to read it, and I was totally fine with that, but the people Patti and I were mentoring as we traveled the globe were the audience that pulled on my heart. I wanted to talk to young men and women who were not hung up in some sort of religious system. From that point on, it was game on. Whether or not I accomplished that with this devo is yet to be seen.

I had a group of people I called the "Devo Club," who read the stuff I was emailing them weekly. Their faces were the ones I pictured when I was writing. Some of them periodically commented and offered suggestions. All of them encouraged me to keep going forward. Taryn Mast, Rocio Doyle, Darci Simpson, Jennifer Goeddertz, Megan Dietrich, Sara Hansen, Dennis Gable, Sarah Lapp Clements, Ashley Higgins, Erika Baldwin, and Kellen Gorbett. Thanks guys! I love you people dearly!

But there were two other members of the Devo Club who gave me feedback on a daily basis. Kayla and Andrea journaled their responses to each day's lesson and basically allowed me to peek into their hearts as they were processing the material. I can't even begin to explain how that kept me going!

Kayla Phillips Hindes was the voice of an angel. She reeks of encouragement anyway, but she really honed her craft when I needed it the most! Thanks baby. I'll owe you forever.

Andrea Gosselin jumped in during the editing process. She made her deeply vulnerable thoughts available to me on a daily basis. What a gift you are, woman! I love what you have with the Lord!

I have had two editors with this project, Erika and David. Erika Baldwin is a true spiritual daughter, but also an amazing wife to Bradley and a committed mother to Hannah and Luke. What it cost her to edit this project is a debt I'll never be able to repay. The Lord spoke clearly to me that she was to be my editor long before I asked her. Patti and I prayed hard about it. We knew this would be a drain on her family. Erika and I were in constant communication throughout the process—a time I'll always cherish. She was perfect for me. She clarified my scribbling without me having to lose my voice. That was what I wanted. That is what I got. Thanks babe! Love you! xo

David Reyes is a busy man. Too busy actually, but he volunteered to be the final eyes before we published ***RAW TALKS WITH WISDOM – Not Your Grandma's Devo***. His gorgeous wife Catherine (now carrying twins) and precious daughter Liv have patiently shared their David throughout this effort. David is a good son. He's served when he really didn't have the time or energy to do it. I'm grateful for his love and devotion. Thanks dude! xo

Once we decided to test readership with an email version of ***RAW TALKS WITH WISDOM – Not Your Grandma's Devo***, it simply would not have happened without Allison Johnston. She basically said, "I'll handle it," and that is exactly what she did. Allison would disappear for a week and then show up and say, "Look at this!" It was awesome! She also took all the pictures we used in the email version. She is the epitome of a spiritual daughter. Perfection really. Love you so much. xo

Jon Egan (my son by marriage) massaged the pics to make the images what we needed them to be. He's the one that has produced most of the graphics and set the overall ambience for the project. He also designed the cover and the Title Page. Again, he just fixed stuff. He always does. What a gift you are to God's people and to me. xo

And then there are the thousands of people who have allowed Patti and I to speak into their lives. I know what I know, and have learned what I have learned, because people were willing to ask me what I thought, and then give me space in their lives to work it out with them.

As I spoke, ministered, discipled, pastored, mentored, and tried to love, I learned a lot about people and probably even more about myself. Even when the stuff coming out of my mouth wasn't too good, most have loved on me well throughout the seasons. I do not deserve all the ways in which I have been honored. Not in the least. Thank you for your trust. I love you all.

And Lord, thank you for your patience, mercy, and unfailing love. You've changed me... from the inside out.

Thank you for everything! I am a blessed man!

Mike
2013

AUTHOR

Mike Paschall was born in Pine Bluff, Arkansas, but raised in Texas. He is a graduate of the University of Arkansas-Fayetteville with a BSEd. He also graduated from Southwestern Baptist Theological Seminary in Ft. Worth, Texas with an MDiv. Mike has served as pastor at numerous churches since 1987 and currently serves as pastor in the United Methodist Church. Mike and Patti were married in 1977. They have two daughters (Nicole, married to Steven Brewer, and Paige, married to Jon Egan) and six grandchildren (Isabel Rose, Jones Michael, Lewis Christian, Grace Irene, Esther Jane, and William Michael) who all live in Colorado Springs, CO. Mike loves any opportunity to mentor young pastors, missionaries, men and women who are passionate about ministry and Kingdom. He also loves preaching, teaching, and writing about the things of God. He is also particularly fond of a good hang with family, a cigar with a great friend, his Indian motorcycle, and an occasional trip to the golf course.

"David once told his son, Solomon, "Wisdom is the principle thing." I think every son craves a father that knows and lives that truth. Mike has taken me (and so many others) under his wing as a son and daily allowed me to grow by experiencing his wisdom, which was earned through all types of joys and sorrows. Wisdom IS the principle thing, and Mike models that by the way he lives, leads, shares and writes!" David Brown - Minister to Youth, Bella Vista Baptist Church, Bella Vista, AR.

"This devo is made most powerful by the man that lives the words every day. Mike Paschall's insights are a testament to a life worth the journey. More than a collection of daily readings--but a lifetime of wisdom, love, and challenge poured onto these pages. RAW TALKS WITH WISDOM will provoke you, inspire you, and make you scratch your head a bit. Often challenging the status quo that was lodged in my spirit, this devo led me to examine fully, wonder longer, and love deeper." - Allison Johnston - COO at Umba "an e-commerce platform for handmade goods," Atlanta, GA.

"Paschall is one of my best friends. Actually more than that, he's my priest. It's usually to him I go when I need a safe place to land my failures. I normally find brutal truth dripping with amazing grace. Regarding this book, it's become one my favorite daily meditations. Mike writes like he lives - vulnerable, honest, and real. WARNING, this book isn't for the staunchly, overly religious, or spiritual know-it-alls. It's a devotional for regular folks, just like us..." Michael Hindes - coach, teacher, trainer, father, President of Kingdom Inc. & MRH Consulting, Atlanta, GA.

"Real, Raw, Biblical, Wise - did I say Raw? Yep - a lot like Mike, is this daily devo he's written, and it's what I love about it (and him). I've known Mike for over 25 years, and one of the things you can count in from him is that he'll tell it to ya straight - no song and dance - no shifting shadows - no wondering "what did he mean by that?" What's best, however, is that his straight talk comes from a place of wisdom, knowledge, experience, and love. There are few people in the planet whose opinion I value more, so just subscribe to the damn devo and read it! Good stuff!" David Johnson – Sr. Pastor at Church of the Open Door, author of *The Subtle Power of Spiritual Abuse*, Maple Grove, MN.

"Mike Paschall is my friend... this Devo is a frank, edgy communication of truths from the heart of God. I love Mike because of his honesty and transparency. If Jesus were talking to his disciples, or to the people of the day, I think he would smile at the conversational communications of this son. If you want a normal religious devotional reading, there are many available... but for those that have embarked on an honest difficult journey with a living Christ... I recommend Mike's Devo's... they will leave you thinking, crying, laughing and challenged." Dr. Bob Nichols - pastoral coach, counselor, teacher, Bellingham, WA

"Mike Paschall's mental and spiritual meanderings are thought provoking and interesting. Mike, who pastored mainstream churches in the past, presents a first hand account of religion, as some of us knew it, with a modern dose of common sense and the realization that all things change and deserve a re-look. Agree with Mike or not you will never be bored and his thoughts will cause you to think. Today's Christianity is due a new look and Christians owe it to themselves and others to use the critical thinking skills God gave us all." Rev. Paula Brown - A true West Texas girl, political purveyor, and forever poster-child of the 60's, Moody, TX.

"If it is real bread from God you want you have picked up the right book. Mike is a very real minister of the gospel that knows what you need when you wake up and you are starving for God to give you a Word for your life. Mike will blast you in the heart with his unique gifted use of language. Mike is one of the most important friends I have in the world. I have known Mike for over twenty-five years as one of my accountability friends. When I need a word from God, in a language that can only come from the Holy Spirit, I call Mike. He is truly gifted with speaking a tongue that you will understand. His devotional guides will guide you to the throne of God." Bart McMillan – Business Chaplain, President of Life's Lesson's Ministries, Gainesville, GA.

"As someone who has rarely done daily devotions, I did not know if I would keep up or stick with it. I've done both, and have thoroughly enjoyed and benefited from these daily "nuggets" of wisdom. These writings are insightful and thought provoking. I look forward to my devotion time every day." David Taylor - Senior Academic Consultant at a large private university, married father-of-two, McGregor, TX.

"Mike's devotionals are open, honest and refreshing. But most of all they are unfiltered by the spirit of "religion" that has invaded so much of biblical teaching in the world today. His desire for us to know the real Jesus is apparent in all that is included in this work. Whether you are a committed follower of Jesus Christ or seeking in your spiritual journey, I recommend this book for you." Barry Strickland - Texas Director of New Wilderness Adventures, Lancaster, TX.

"One of the characteristics of Mike Paschall that I greatly respect is his direct approach. He has a gift for unpacking principles and truths from God's Word and putting them in down-to-earth and in-your-face words that make it impossible to wiggle away from their weightiness. In RAW TALKS WITH WISDOM, Mike shares a daily dose of truth, without the sugar coating, that will lead you to a deeper relationship with God." Stephanie Pridgen - Missionary Church Administrator for International Christian Assembly, Kiev, Ukraine.

"Nothing strikes of more importance to me than 'a real Christian' and by that I mean a raw, lay it out on the table, I've made mistakes, and this is who I am Christian. We are called to make disciples and I truly believe we can't do that until we are real with each other. And that is why RAW TALKS WITH WISDOM is truly amazing. They are as real and raw as it gets. I truly believe the "church" is afraid to talk that way, but through Mike and his devos I have been able to face obstacles that I can assure you are not pretty or clean, but that is life and thank God somebody like Mike is not afraid to speak right to the heart of what life is really all about!" Taryn Mast – Performance Coach, San Diego, CA.

"To know Mike is to love him dearly or not at all, mostly because he leaves very little margin for misunderstanding. RAW TALKS WITH WISDOM is beautiful for that very reason; it is a heartfelt journey through the book of Proverbs that will lead you gracefully into a deeper relationship with Wisdom. 'In The Pages' offers an opportunity for each reader to work through the details as their story collides with God's story through the scriptures. If you are looking for a devotional that will make you feel safe, this isn't it. If you're searching for a daily opportunity to be honest with yourself and with God, then dive in... just keep in mind, this isn't your grandma's devo!" Dennis Gable – A multi-faceted, uniquely gifted Kingdom communicator who lives with his

gorgeous wife and beautiful children in Phoenix, AZ.

www.ingramcontent.com/pod-product-compliance
Lightning Source LLC
Chambersburg PA
CBHW021950290426
44108CB00012B/1015